PRINCIPAL COINS
OF THE ROMANS

PRINCIPAL COINS
OF THE ROMANS

VOLUME III
THE DOMINATE
AD294-498

R.A.G. CARSON

Published for
The Trustees of the British Museum by
British Museum Publications Limited

British Library Cataloguing in Publication Data
Carson, Robert Andrew Glendinning
   Principal coins of the Romans.
   Vol. 3: The Dominate AD 294–498.
   1. Coins, Roman
   I. Title
   737.4'9'37   CJ833

   ISBN 0 7141 0853 7
   ISBN 0 7141 0839 1 Set of 3 vols

© 1981, The Trustees of the British Museum
ISBN 0 7141 0839 1 *the set*
ISBN 0 7141 0844 8 *Volume 1*
ISBN 0 7141 0852 9 *Volume 2*
ISBN 0 7141 0853 7 *Volume 3*
Published by British Museum Publications Ltd
6 Bedford Square, London WC1B 3RA

Designed by Harry Green
Set in 10 on 11pt Bembo
Printed in Great Britain by Balding and Mansell

Jacket
Left (from top to bottom): 1177, aureus, obv., rev.;
1599, solidus, obv., rev.; *right*: 1359, medallion, obv.

Contents

C J 8 33
.C 32
v. 3
GESW

1 First Tetrarchy (post-reform) AD 294–305

The coinage which had been produced for the First Tetrarchy created by the appointment of Constantius Chlorus and Galerius as Caesars to the two Augusti Maximian and Diocletian respectively was superseded by a new coinage introduced by the reform of AD 294. The aureus continued to be struck at a standard of 60 to the pound, and sometimes was so marked by the Greek numeral Ϛ, a form of Ξ (=60). A new silver coin of fineness about 98 per cent was introduced, struck on a standard of 96 to the pound, and sometimes so marked XCVI, at a theoretical weight of 3.41 gm. A new denomination with laureate obverse was struck in argentiferous bronze on a standard of about 32 to the pound, with a weight of about 10 gm., and by tradition termed a follis. The argentiferous bronze antoninianus of the earlier coinage appears to have been used as a subsidiary denomination but was shortly replaced by a similar radiate coin, in bronze only. Additionally a smaller fractional bronze coin with laureate obverse was struck at an average weight of 1.30 gm. The correct names for the subsidiary coins, and their denominational relations remain the subject of controversy.

The mints of the pre-reform period continued to be active with the exception of Tripolis. After the reconquest of Britain in AD 296 the mint at London was retained to strike the new Tetrarchic coinage, and new mints for the reformed coinage were opened at Aquileia in Italy, at Carthage in North Africa, at Nicomedia in Asia, at Alexandria in Egypt, and from AD 298 at Thessalonica in the Balkans, and at Serdica from AD 304. The practice of placing the signature of the mint on coinage of all metals now became much more widespread, though some issues still continued to be unmarked.

1150 Follis London, *c.* AD 297

Obv. IMP MAXIMIANVS PI FE AVG. Head, laureate, r.
Rev. GENIO POPVLI ROMANI. Genius standing l., modius on head, and chlamys over l. shoulder, holding patera in r. hand, and cornucopiae in l.; mint-mark, LON.
Æ, 9.36 gm. ↓.

The London mint appears to have issued only folles.

1151 Follis London, *c.* AD 300

Obv. IMP C MAXIMIANVS P F AVG. Bust, laureate, cuirassed, r.
Rev. As No. 1150 but no mint-mark.
Æ, 10.03 gm.

After the first issue of the follis coinage, the mint signature of the London mint was omitted from the coinage.

1152 Medallion Trier, AD 296–7

Obv. FL VAL CONSTANTIVS NOBILISSIMVS C. Bust with lion-skin head-dress, r.
Rev. PIETAS AVGG. Constantius standing r., holding spear in l. hand, and, with r., raising kneeling Britannia; behind him, Victory standing r., holding palm and crowning Constantius with wreath; mint-mark, PTR.
N, 26.80 gm. ↓.

The reverse of this five-aureus piece clearly commemorates the reconquest of Britain by Constantius in AD 296.

1153 Aureus Trier, AD 296–7

Obv. DIOCLETIANVS AVG. Head, laureate, r.
Rev. COMES AVGG. Mars standing r., head l., in
   distyle temple, holding spear and shield;
   mint-mark, TR. N, 4.91 gm. ↑.
This, and the following two coins, form part of the
issue celebrating the reconquest of Britain.

1154 Aureus Trier, AD 296–7

Obv. MAXIMIANVS AVG. Head, laureate, r.
Rev. PACATORES GENTIVM. Emperor standing
   facing, head l., holding branch in r. hand, in
   facing quadriga led by soldier; mint-mark,
   TR. N, 5.07 gm. ↑.

1155 Aureus Trier, AD 296–7

Obv. MAXIMIANVS AVG. Head, laureate, r.
Rev. VIRTVS ILLVRICI. Maximian galloping r.,
   spear downwards; below, galley r.; mint-
   mark, TR. N, 5.34 gm. ↑.

1156 Aureus Trier, AD 302–3

Obv. MAXIMIANVS NOB C. Head, laureate, r.
Rev. SIC X / SIC XX / COS IIII within wreath.
   N, 5.02 gm. ↓.
The reverse commemorates the tenth anniversary
of the appointment of Galerius and Constantius as
Caesars.

1157 Quarter-aureus Trier, AD 303

Obv. MAXIMIANVS N C. Head, laureate, r.
Rev. VOT / IS X / SIC / XX in wreath. N, 1.26 gm. ↑.
This unusual denomination forms part of the
coinage celebrating the tenth anniversary of the
creation of the First Tetrarchy.

1158 Aureus Trier, AD 303

Obv. DIOCLETIANVS P F AVG. Head, laureate, r.
Rev. VOT / XX / SIC / XXX in wreath. N, 5.44 gm. ↓.
Part of the coinage of the First Tetrarchy, recording
the decennalia of the Tetrarchy, and the vicennalian
vows of Diocletian.

1159 Aureus Trier, AD 303

Obv. MAXIMIANVS P F AVG. Head, laureate, r.
Rev. HERCVLI CONSERVATORI. Bust of Hercules r.,
   in lion-skin head-dress; mint-mark, TR.
   N. 5.24 gm. ↓.

In an issue for all four Tetrarchs the reverse type is the bust of a deity. The others are: for Diocletian, Jupiter; for Constantius, Mars; and for Galerius, Sol.

1160 Aureus Trier, AD 303

Obv. CONSTANTIVS NOB C. Head, laureate, r.
Rev. VIRTVS HERCVLI CAESARIS. Constantius riding r., holding spear in r. hand; mint-mark, TR. *AV*, 5.27 gm. ↓.
The reverse inscription emphasises that Hercules was the tutelary deity of Constantius as well as of Maximian.

1161 Argenteus Trier, AD 294

Obv. DIOCLETIANVS AVG. Head, laureate, r.
Rev. VIRTVS MILTVM. The four tetrarchs sacrificing in front of gateway of six-turreted enclosure. *AR*, 2.59 gm. ↑.
An early example of the new silver denomination struck at a standard of 96 to the pound.

1162 Argenteus Trier, AD 295–7

Obv. CONSTANTIVS NOB C. Head, laureate, r.
Rev. VICTORIA SARMAT. As No. 1161; in ex., C. *AR*, 3.18 gm. ↓.
The use of officina letters C and D is similar to that on the earlier antoninianus coinage of Trier for the First Tetrarchy.

1163 Argenteus Trier, AD 300–1

Obv. MAXIMIANVS AVG. Bust, laureate, cuirassed, l.
Rev. VIRTVS MILITVM. As on No. 1161; in ex., club. *AR*, 3.48 gm. ↓.
The club symbol of Hercules is an appropriate mark for Trier, the residence of Maximian Herculius.

1164 Follis Trier, AD 310–11

Obv. IMP DIOCLETIANVS P F AVG. Bust, laureate, cuirassed, r.
Rev. FORTVNAE REDVCI AVGG NN. Fortuna seated l. on wheel, holding rudder in r. hand, and cornucopiae in l; mint-mark, $\frac{|*}{BTR}$.
Æ, 10.06 gm. ↑.
The Fortuna Redux type probably echoes the successful conclusion of Maximian's African campaign, Constantius' Rhineland campaign, and of the Persian campaign of Galerius.

1165 Follis Lyons, AD 303–5

Obv. IMP MAXIMIANVS AVG. Bust, laureate, cuirassed, l.
Rev. GENIO POPVLI ROMANI. Genius standling l., modius on head, and chlamys over l. shoulder, holding patera in r. hand, and cornucopiae in l.; in field l., altar; mint-mark, $\frac{|*}{PLG}$.
Æ, 11.61 gm. ↑.

This mint-mark marks the last issue of the First Tetrarchy at Lyons, and is continued under the Second Tetrarchy. The mint at this time was reduced to a single officina.

1166 Aureus Ticinum, AD 294–5

Obv. FL VAL CONSTANTIVS NOB CAES. Bust, laureate, draped, cuirassed, r.
Rev. PROVIDENTIA DEORVM. Providentia seated l., holding wand over globe, and sceptre. N, 5.45 gm. ↓.

1167 Follis fraction Ticinum, AD 294–5

Obv. MAXIMIANVS AVG. Head, laureate, r.
Rev. VTILITAS PVBLICA. Utilitas standing facing, head l.; mint-mark, T. Æ, 1.44 gm. ↓.

1168 Argenteus Ticinum, AD 300

Obv. MAXIMIANVS AVG. Head, laureate, r.
Rev. XCVI in wreath; mint-mark, T. Æ, 3.01 gm. ↑.

1169 Follis Ticinum, AD 300–3

Obv. IMP DIOCLETIANVS P F AVG. Head, laureate, r.

Rev. SACRA MONET AVGG ET CAESS NOSTR. Moneta standing l., holding scales and cornucopiae; mint-mark, ST. Æ, 8.85 gm. ↓.

1170 Aureus Ticinum, AD 303

Obv. DIOCLETIANVS AVGVSTVS. Head, laureate, r.
Rev. XX / DIOCL / ETIAN / I AVG within wreath; mint-mark, SMT. N, 5.64 gm. ↓.

1171 Aureus Aquileia, AD 294–303

Obv. CONSTANTIVS CAES. Head, laureate, r.
Rev. COMITES AVGG ET CAESS NNNN. The Dioscuri standing facing, heads r., with stars above helmets; each holds staff in r. hand, and chlamys over l. arm; mint-mark, AQ. N, 5.24 gm. ↑.

Aquileia was one of the new mints opened to strike the reform coinage.

1172 Aureus Aquileia, AD 294–303

Obv. DIOCLETIANVS P F AVG. Head, laureate, r.
Rev. CONCORDIA AVGG ET CAESS NNNN. Concordia seated l., holding patera and double-cornucopiae; mint-mark, AQ. N, 5.32 gm. ↑.

1173 Argenteus Aquileia, AD 294–5

Obv. DIOCLETIANVS AVG. Head, laureate, r.
Rev. XCVI in wreath; mint-mark, AQ.
 Æ, 2.64 gm. ↓.

1174 Aureus Aquileia, AD 303

Obv. MAXIMIANVS P F AVG. Head, laureate, r.
Rev. VOT / XX / AVGG within wreath, at foot of
 which, eagle. *N*, 5.42 gm. ↑.
Part of the coinage celebrating Maximian's
vicennalia. The eagle (*aquila*) on the reverse is a
punning symbol for the mint of Aquileia.

1175 Aureus Aquileia, AD 303–5

Obv. MAXIMIANVS CAESAR. Head, laureate, r.
Rev. IOVI CONSERVATORI. Jupiter standing l.,
 holding thunderbolt and sceptre; mint-
 mark, SMAQ. *N* 5.36 gm. ↑.

1176 Follis Aquileia, AD 303

Obv. MAXIMIANVS P F AVG. Head, laureate, r.
Rev. SACR MONET AVGG ET CAESS NOSTR. Moneta
 standing l., holding scales and cornucopiae;
 mint-mark, ⌊VI̶ / AQP.
 Æ, 9.41 gm. ↓.

There is a suggestion that the numeral VI in the field
of the reverse marks this coinage as the sixth issue of
folles at this mint.

1177 Aureus Rome, AD 294–5

Obv. MAXIMIANVS AVG. Head, laureate, r.
Rev. COMITATVS AVGG. Diocletian and Maximian
 riding l; both raising r. hand; the nearer
 holds short sceptre in l; mint-mark, PR.
 N, 7.24 gm. ↓.

1178 Aureus Rome, AD 294–5

Obv. MAXIMIANVS CAES. Head, laureate, r.
Rev. VIRTVS MILITVM. Camp-gate with open door,
 and eight turrets, mint-mark, PR.
 N, 5.68 gm. ↑.

1179 Argenteus Rome, AD 294

Obv. DIOCLETIANVS AVG. Head, laureate, r.
Rev. PROVIDENTIA AVGG. The four Tetrarchs
 sacrificing over tripod before gate in six-
 turreted enclosure; mint-mark, R.
 Æ, 3.04 gm. ↑.

1180 Argenteus Rome, AD 295–7

Obv. CONSTANTIVS CAES. Head, laureate, r.
Rev. VIRTVS MILITVM. As No. 1179; in ex., *Γ*.
 Æ, 3.25 gm. ↓.

1181 Follis fraction Rome, AD 297–8

Obv. FL VAL CONSTANTIVS NOB C. Bust, radiate,
   draped, cuirassed, r.
Rev. VOT / XX / Γ in wreath. Æ, 2.69 gm. ↑.

1182 Follis Rome, AD 302–3

Obv. IMP C MAXIMIANVS P F AVG. Head, laureate, r.
Rev. SACRA MON VRB AVGG ET CAESS NN. Moneta
   standing l., holding scales and cornucopiae;
   mint-mark, ⎮*.
                RS
   Æ, 10.38 gm. ↑.

1183 Aureus Carthage, AD 296–7

Obv. DIOCLETIANVS P F AVG. Head, laureate, r.
Rev. FELIX ADVENT AVGG NN. Africa standing
   facing, head l., in elephant-skin head-dress,
   holding standard in r. hand, and tusk in l.; at
   feet l., lion couched on bull; mint-mark, PK.
   Ν, 4.66 gm. ↑.

The new mint at Carthage was opened in
connection with Maximian's campaign against the
Quinquegentiani in AD 296–7.

1184 Argenteus Carthage, AD 296–8

Obv. CONSTANTIVS CAES. Head, laureate, r.
Rev. F ADVENT AVGG NN. As No. 1183; in ex., T.
   Æ, 3.52 gm. ↑.

1185 Follis Carthage, AD 298–9

Obv. MAXIMIANVS NOB CAES. Head, laureate, r.
Rev. SALVIS AVGG ET CAESS FEL KART. Carthage
   standing facing, head l., holding fruits in
   both hands; in ex., Δ. Æ, 8.82 gm. ↑.
In the follis coinage of Carthage one officina was
allotted to each Tetrarch in order of seniority. Here
Δ, the fourth, is given to Galerius, the most junior.

1186 Argenteus Carthage, AD 300

Obv. MAXIMIANVS AVG. Head, laureate, r.
Rev. XC / VI in wreath. Æ, 3.45 gm. ↓.

1187 Aureus Carthage, AD 303

Obv. MAXIMIANVS P F AVG. Head, laureate, r.
Rev. HERCVLI COMITI AVGG ET CAESS NN. Hercules
   standing r., r. hand on club, and holding
   apple and lion-skin in l.; mint-mark, PK.
   Ν, 5.57 gm. ↓.

1188 Follis fraction Carthage, AD 300

Obv. IMP C DIOCLETIANVS P F AVG. Bust, radiate, draped, cuirassed, r.
Rev. VOT / XX in wreath; mint-mark, FK. Æ, 3.17 gm. ↓.
These bronze fractions issued on the occasion of the vicennalia of the Augusti are signed FK = *Felix Karthago.*

1189 Aureus Siscia, AD 295–6

Obv. MAXIMIANVS AVGVSTVS. Head, laureate, r.
Rev. HERCVLI PACIFERO. Hercules standing facing, head l.; holding branch in r. hand, and club and lion-skin in l.; mint-mark, *SIS. N, 5.15 gm. ↓.

1190 Aureus Siscia, AD 295–6

Obv. DIOCLETIANVS AVGVSTVS. Head, laureate, r.
Rev. IOVI VICTORI. Jupiter standing l., holding Victory on globe in r. hand, and sceptre in l.; mint-mark, *SIS. N, 5.01 gm. ↓.

1191 Aureus Siscia, AD 295–6

Obv. MAXIMIANVS NOB C. Head, laureate, r.
Rev. MARTI PROPVGNATORI. Mars advancing r., holding spear and shield; mint-mark, *SIS. N, 5.31 gm. ↑.

1192 Argenteus Siscia, AD 294–5

Obv. DIOCLETIANVS AVG. Head, laureate, r.
Rev. VICTORIA SARMAT. The four tetrarchs sacrificing over tripod before archway in eight-turreted enclosure. Æ, 3.37 gm. ↓.

1193 Argenteus Siscia, AD 295

Obv. MAXIMIANVS NOB C. Head, laureate, r.
Rev. VICTORIA AVGG. As No. 1192, but six turrets; mint-mark, *SIS. Æ, 2.83 gm. ↓.

1194 Follis Siscia, AD 300

Obv. CONSTANTIVS NOB CAES. Head, laureate, r.
Rev. GENIO POPVLI ROMANI. Genius standing l., modius on head, and chlamys over l. shoulder, holding patera and cornucopiae; mint-mark, $\frac{S|B}{XXISIS}$.
Æ, 10.47 gm. ↑.
For the varying letters placed in the left field of the reverse no convincing explanation has yet been advanced.

1195 Argenteus Serdica, AD 303–5

Obv. MAXIMIANVS AVG. Head, laureate, r.
Rev. VIRTVS MILITVM. Camp-gate with three
   turrets and open door; mint-mark, ·SM·SDΔ·.
   Æ, 3.29 gm. ↑.
The mint at Serdica was re-opened about AD 300.

1196 Follis Serdica, AD 303–5

Obv. GAL VAL MAXIMIANVS NOB CAES. Head,
   laureate, r.
Rev. GENIO POPVLI ROMANI. Genius standing l.,
   with modius on head and chlamys over l.
   shoulder, holding patera and cornucopiae;
   mint-mark, $\dfrac{|\ \varDelta}{\text{SM·SD}}$·.
   Æ, 10.22 gm. ↑.

1197 Aureus Thessalonica, AD 300–3

Obv. DIOCLETIANVS P F AVG. Head, laureate, r.
Rev. IOVI CONSERVATORI. Jupiter standing l.,
   holding thunderbolt and sceptre; at foot
   left, eagle; mint-mark, $\dfrac{|\ \mathstrut \text{ᴢ}}{\text{T·S·}}$.

   N, 5.13 gm. ↑.
The mint of Thessalonica was opened some years
after the coinage reform. The numeral ᴢ = Ξ, in the
reverse fields marks the coin as struck on a standard
of 60 to the pound.

1198 Aureus Thessalonica, AD 300–3

Obv. MAXIMIANVS NOB CAES. Head, laureate, r.
Rev. CONSVL CAESS. Galerius in consular dress
   standing l., holding globe and short
   sceptre; mint-mark, $\dfrac{|\ \text{ᴢ}}{\text{T·S·}}$.

   N, 5.36 gm. ↑.
Both the Caesars, Constantius and Galerius, were
consuls in AD 300 and again in AD 302.

1199 Argenteus Thessalonica, AD 302

Obv. MAXIMIANVS NOB C. Head, laureate, r.
Rev. VIRTVS MILITVM. Camp-gate with three
   turrets and open door; mint-mark, ·T·S· Γ.
   Æ, 3.51 gm. ↑.

1200 Follis Thessalonica, AD 302–3

Obv. FL VAL CONSTANTIVS NOB CAES. Head,
   laureate, r.
Rev. GENIO POPVLI ROMANI. Genius standing l.,
   modius on head and chlamys over l.
   shoulder, holding patera and cornucopiae;
   mint-mark, $\dfrac{|\ \Gamma}{\text{·T·S·}}$.
   Æ, 10.28 gm. ↓.

1201 Follis Heraclea, AD 296–7

Obv. IMP C C VAL DIOCLETIANVS P F AVG. Head, laureate, r.
Rev. As No. 1196, but mint-mark, HTΔ.
Æ, 9.33 gm. ↑.

1202 Medallion Nicomedia, AD 294

Obv. IMP C C VAL DIOCLETIANVS P F AVG. Head, bare, r.
Rev. IOVI CONSERVATORI. Jupiter standing facing, head l., with chlamys draped over r. arm, holding Victory on globe, and sceptre; at foot l., eagle with wreath in beak; mint-mark, SMN. N, 53.5 gm. ↑.
An example of a ten-aureus medallion.

1203 Aureus Nicomedia, AD 294

Obv. MAXIMIANVS P F AVG. Head, laureate, r.
Rev. HERCVLI VICTORI. Hercules standing facing, head r., leaning r. hand on club, and holding apple and lion-skin in l.; mint-mark, SMNVI. N, 6.71 gm. ↑.

1204 Follis Nicomedia, AD 294–5

Obv. IMP C C VAL DIOCLETIANVS P F AVG. Head, laureate, r.
Rev. GENIO POPVLI ROMANI. As No. 1201, but mint-mark, SMNB. Æ, 10.43 gm. ↑.

1205 Aureus Nicomedia, AD 295

Obv. CONSTANTIVS NOB CAES. Head, laureate, r.
Rev. HERCVLI VICTORI. As No. 1203, but mint-mark, ·SMN. N, 5.37 gm. ↑.

1206 Aureus Nicomedia, AD 295

Obv. MAXIMIANVS NOB CAES. Head, laureate, r.
Rev. IOVI CONSERVATORI. Jupiter standing l., chlamys over shoulders, holding thunderbolt and sceptre; mint-mark, ·SMN. N, 5.34 gm. ↑.

1207 Argenteus Nicomedia, AD 296–7

Obv. MAXIMIANVS AVG. Head, laureate, r.
Rev. VICTORIAE SARMATICAE. Camp-gate with
  four turrets and open doors; above, star;
  mint-mark, SMNΓ. Æ, 3.33 gm. ↑.

1208 Aureus Nicomedia, AD 303–4

Obv. DIOCLETIANVS AVGVSTVS. Head, laureate, r.
Rev. XX / DIOCL / ETIAN / I AVG within wreath;
  mint-mark, SMN. N, 5.35 gm. ↓.

1209 Argenteus Cyzicus, AD 294–5

Obv. MAXIMIANVS CAESAR. Head, laureate, r.
Rev. VIRTVS MILITVM. The four Tetrarchs
  sacrificing over tripod before archway in
  six-turreted enclosure; mint-mark, CM.
  Æ, 3.07 gm. ↑.

1210 Follis Cyzicus, AD 297–9

Obv. FL VAL CONSTANTIVS NOB CAES. Head,
  laureate, r.
Rev. GENIO AVGG ET CAESARVM NN. Genius as on
  No. 1201; mint-mark, K Δ. Æ, 8.81 gm. ↑.
This unusual inscription accompanying the Genius
reverse is used only for the Caesars. For the Augusti
the inscription is the normal GENIO POPVLI ROMANI.

1211 Follis fraction Cyzicus, AD 295–9

Obv. GAL VAL MAXIMIANVS NOB CAES. Bust,
  radiate, cuirassed, r.
Rev. CONCORDIA MILITVM. Galerius standing r.,
  receiving Victory on globe from Jupiter
  standing l., holding sceptre; mint-mark, K Γ.
  Æ, 3.13 gm. ↑.

1212 Aureus Antioch, AD 294–5

Obv. CONSTANTIVS NOB CAES. Head, laureate, r.
Rev. HERCVLI CONS CAES. Hercules standing
  facing, head l., leaning r. hand on club, and
  holding apples and lion-skin in l.; mint-
  mark, SMA₃. N, 5.32 gm. ↑.

1213 Aureus Antioch, AD 294–5

Obv. MAXIMIANVS NOB CAES. Head, laureate, r.
Rev. IOVI CONS CAES. Jupiter standing facing, head
  l., chlamys hanging from shoulders, holding
  thunderbolt and sceptre; at foot l., eagle;
  mint-mark, SMA₃. N, 5.33 gm. ↓.

1214 Argenteus Antioch, AD 298

Obv. MAXIMIANVS CAESAR. Head, laureate, r.
Rev. VIRTVS MILITVM. Camp-gate with three
  turrets and open door; mint-mark, ·ANTH·.
  Æ, 3.14 gm. ↓.

1215 Follis Antioch, AD 300–1

Obv. IMP C DIOCLETIANVS P F AVG. Head, laureate, r.
Rev. GENIO POPVLI ROMANI. As No. 1201, but
mint-mark, $\frac{\text{K}\,|\,\text{S}}{\text{V}}$.
$\overline{\text{ANT}}$

Æ, 11.17 gm. ↓.

The formula KV on the reverse may be a parallel to
the XXI formula, e.g. on No. 1194 above. This,
however, requires acceptance of a mixed formula:
K (Greek numeral) = 20 sestertii, and V (Latin
numeral) = 5 denarii.

1216 Aureus Alexandria, AD 294–6

Obv. DIOCLETIANVS AVG. Head, laureate, r.
Rev. IOVI CONSER AVGG. As no. 1213, but
mint-mark, $\frac{|\ast}{\text{ALE}}$.

N, 5.31 gm. ↑.

The new reformed coinage was issued at Alexandria
from AD 294, but for three years it was accompanied by issues of the traditional Alexandrian
tetradrachm.

1217 Aureus Alexandria, AD 295–6

Obv. DOMITIANVS AVG. Head, laureate, r.
Rev. VICTOI AVG. Victory advancing l., holding
wreath and palm. N, 5.41 gm. ↑.

The usurper Domitius Domitianus issued both gold
and folles from the mint of Alexandria.

1218 Follis Alexandria, AD 295–6

Obv. IMP C L DOMITIVS DOMITIANVS AVG. Head,
laureate, r.
Rev. GENIO POPVLI ROMANI. Genius standing l.,
modius on head and chlamys over l.
shoulder, holding patera and cornucopiae;
at foot l., eagle; mint-mark, $\frac{|\text{B}}{\text{ALE}}$.

Æ, 10.38 gm. ↑.

1219 Argenteus Alexandria, AD 295–6

Obv. MAXIMIANVS AVG. Head, laureate, r.
Rev. VIRTVS MILITVM. Camp-gate with three
turrets and no doors; mint-mark, $\frac{|\text{Γ}}{\text{ALE}}$.

Æ, 3.16 gm. ↑.

1220 Follis Alexandria, AD 301

Obv. IMP C MAXIMIANVS P F AVG. Head, laureate, r.
Rev. GENIO POPVLI ROMANI. As No. 1218, but no
eagle, and mint-mark, $\frac{\text{XX}\,|\,\text{I}}{\text{ALE}}$.

Æ, 9.79 gm. ↓.

1221 Follis Alexandria, AD 304

Obv. GAL VAL MAXIMIANVS NOB CAES. Head,
 laureate, r.
Rev. IOVI CONS CAES. Jupiter standing l.,
 holding Victory on globe and sceptre;
 mint-mark, | A
              S | P .
              ALE
 Æ, 11.96 gm. ↑.

2 Second and Third Tetrarchies and aftermath, AD 305–313

The coinage is dealt with here as one group, as in some cases rulers continue with the same titulature in more than one period, and in view of the general complexity of the history of the period.

On the abdication of Diocletian and Maximian in AD 305 a Second Tetrarchy was created, consisting of Constantius and Galerius as Augusti, and Severus and Maximinus Daza as the respective Caesars. The death of Constantius in AD 306 resulted in the creation of a Third Tetrarchy in which Severus became Augustus and Constantine was appointed his Caesar in the West, but this arrangement was quickly disrupted by the revolt of Maxentius in Italy, the return of Maximian as an Augustus, and the elevation of Constantine to Augustus in late AD 307. At the conference of Carnuntum in AD 308 Diocletian endeavoured to restore Tetrarchic unity by appointing Licinius as fellow Augustus to Galerius to replace Severus who had been killed, maintaining Maximinus as Caesar, demoting Constantine to the rank of Caesar, refusing to recognise Maxentius, and insisting on Maximian's withdrawal as an active Augustus. Galerius endeavoured to placate Constantine and Maximinus with the title *Filius Augustorum*, but Constantine continued to regard himself as an Augustus, though Maximinus used the title until at least AD 310. Control of the empire east of the Bosphorus passed to Maximinus on the death of Galerius in AD 311, while Licinius held the Balkan provinces and Constantine, by his defeat of Maxentius in AD 312, controlled the western provinces. Licinius ultimately gained control of the eastern provinces on the death of Maximinus in AD 313.

A number of changes took place in the pattern of mints active in this period. When Domitius Alexander revolted in North Africa in AD 308, Maxentius transferred the mint organisation of Carthage to a new mint at Ostia. In the Balkans Thessalonica, which had closed in AD 303, was re-opened in AD 308 to replace the mint at Serdica which was closed in that year.

The coinage system also underwent some changes. In AD 310 Constantine introduced a new gold denomination, the solidus, on a standard of 72 to the pound, with an average weight of 4.50 gm., but the aureus contined to be issued by mints not under the control of Constantine. The silver argenteus continued to be issued but much less frequently than under the First Tetrarchy. It is now recognised the reduction in weight of the argentiferous bronze follis between AD 307 and 313 was not simply a continuous decline, but took the form of a series of step-changes from 32 to 36, 40, 48 and finally 72 folles to the pound.

1222 Follis London, AD 305–7

Obv. MAXIMINVS NOBILISSIMVS CAES. Bust, laureate, draped, cuirassed, r.
Rev. GENIO POPVLI ROMANI. Genius standing l., modius on head, and chlamys over l. shoulder, holding patera in r. hand, and cornucopiae in l. Æ, 8.84 gm. ↓.

On the follis coinage of the Second and Third Tetrarchies at London the mint-signature continued to be omitted.

1223 Follis London, AD 307

Obv. D N MAXIMIANO P F S AVG. Bust, laureate, draped, cuirassed, r.
Rev. HERCVLI CONSERVATORI. Hercules standing facing, head r., resting r. hand on club, and holding bow and lion-skin in r.; mint-mark, PLN. Æ, 7.47 gm. ↓.

The abbreviation S for *senior* in the *obv.* inscription marks this as coinage for Maximian as Augustus for the second time. From this date onwards the coinage of London carries the mint-signature.

1224 Follis London, AD 312–13

Obv. CONSTANTINVS P AVG. Bust in laureate helmet, cuirassed, l., holding spear and shield.
Rev. SECVRITAS AVGG. Securitas standing l., raising r. hand to head, and leaning l. elbow on column; mint-mark, $*|$.
Æ, 4.24 gm. ↓.   PLN

1225 Aureus Trier, AD 305–6

Obv. MAXIMIANVS P F AVG. Head, laureate, r.
Rev. IOVI CONSERVATORI AVGG ET CAESS NN. Jupiter seated l., holding thunderbolt in r. hand, and sceptre in l.; mint-mark, TR. N, 5.48 gm. ↓.
The dating of this issue of Galerius is confirmed by the use of the reverse by the other members of the Second Tetrarchy.

1226 Follis Trier, AD 305–7

Obv. D N MAXIMIANO FELICISSIMO SEN AVG. Bust, laureate, in imperial mantle r., holding branch in r. hand, and mappa in l.
Rev. PROVIDENTIA DEORVM QVIES AVGG. Providentia standing l., extending r. hand to Quies standing l., holding branch in r. hand, and sceptre in l.; mint-mark, S | F .
Æ, 10.89 gm. ↑.   PTR
The reverse refers to the abdication of Diocletian and Maximian in AD 305 as does the title *Senior Augustus* on the obverse.

1227 Aureus Trier, AD 306–7

Obv. CONSTANTINVS NOB C. Head, laureate, r.
Rev. PRINCIPI IVVENTVTIS. Constantine holding spear in r. hand, standing l. between two standards; mint-mark, TR. N, 5.30 gm. ↓.
Coinage of Constantine as Caesar in the Third Tetrarchy.

1228 Argenteus Trier, AD 306–7

Obv. As No. 1227.
Rev. VIRTVS MILITVM. Gateway with open door, and four turrets; mint-mark, PTR.
Æ, 3.47 gm. ↓.

1229 Follis Trier, AD 307

Obv. FL VAL CONSTANTINVS NOB C. Bust, laureate, cuirassed, r.
Rev. MARTI PATRI PROPVGNATORI. Mars advancing r., holding spear and shield; mint-mark, S | A .
PTR
Æ, 6.53 gm. ↓.

1230 Half-argenteus Trier, AD 307–8

Obv. IMP CONSTANTINVS P F AVG. Bust, laureate,
cuirassed, r.
Rev. VIRTVS MILITVM. Gateway with open door,
and four turrets; mint-mark, TR.
Æ, 1.49 gm. ↑.
In late AD 307 Constantine was appointed Augustus
by Maximian, his father-in-law and Senior
Augustus.

1231 Half-argenteus Trier, AD 307–8

Obv. FAVSTAE NOBILISSIMAE FEMINAE. Bust, draped l.
Rev. VENVS FELIX. Venus seated l., holding globe
in r. hand, and palm in l.; mint-mark, TR.
Æ, 1.20 gm. ↓.
The reverse is an obvious reference to Constantine's
marriage to Fausta, daughter of Maximian, in late
AD 307.

1232 Follis Trier, AD 307–8

Obv. DIVO CONSTANTIO PIO. Bust, laureate, veiled,
draped, r.
Rev. MEMORIA FELIX. Lighted and garlanded altar;
on either side, an eagle; mint-mark, PTR.
Æ, 5.44 gm. ↓.
Memorial coinage issued by Constantine in honour
of his deified father, Constantius.

1233 Solidus Trier, AD 310–13

Obv. CONSTANTINVS P F AVG. Head, laureate, r.
Rev. GLORIA EXERCITVS GALL. Constantine riding
r., r. hand raised; mint-mark, PTR.
N, 4.54 gm. ↓.
An early example of Constantine's new gold
denomination, the solidus. The reverse honours the
army which had secured Constantine's success
against the Alamanni and the Franks.

1234 Silver Trier, AD 312–13

Obv. IMP MAXIMINVS AVG. Bust, radiate, draped,
cuirassed l., r. hand raised, and holding
globe in l.
Rev. SOLI INVICTO COMITI. Sol, radiate, standing,
head l., in facing quadriga, r. hand raised,
and holding globe and whip in l.; mint-
mark, PTR. Æ, 3.52 gm. ↑.
The denomination is uncertain. The single assay
carried out of a coin of this group indicates that the
fineness is only 25 per cent.

1235 Silver Trier, AD 312–13

Obv. IMP LICINIVS AVG. Bust, laureate, cuirassed, l.,
holding thunderbolt in r. hand, and sceptre
over shoulder in l.
Rev. IOVI CONSERVATORI AVG. Jupiter holding
thunderbolt and sceptre, seated on eagle
standing r., mint-mark, STR. Æ, 3.27 gm. ↑.
cf. comment on No. 1234.

1236 Follis Lyons, AD 307

Obv. D N MAXIMIANO P F S AVG. Bust, laureate, in
imperial mantle, l., holding eagle-tipped
sceptre in r. hand.

Rev. GENIO POPVLI ROMANI. Genius standing l.,
modius on head, and drapery on loins,
holding patera in r. hand, and cornucopiae
in l.; to l., altar; mint-mark, ⎯N⎯.
Æ, 9.00 gm. ↑.   PLG

Coinage of Maximian as Augustus for a second
time.

1237 Follis Lyons, AD 308–9

Obv. IMP C CONSTANTINVS P F AVG. Bust, laureate,
draped, cuirassed, r.

Rev. CONSTANTINO P AVG B R P NAT. Constantine
standing facing, head l., holding globe
and sceptre; mint-mark,   CI|H
Æ, 6.78 gm. ↑.   ⎯S⎯ .
                                   PLG

The concluding portion of the reverse inscription
B R P NAT, expanded as *Bono Rei Publicae Nato*,
suggests that this coinage was produced for
Constantine's birthday on 27 February of this year.
The letters in the field of the reverse may possibly
contain some value notation but, if so, its meaning
remains obscure.

1238 Aureus Ticinum, AD 305–6

Obv. SEVERVS NOB CAES. Head, laureate, r.

Rev. HERCVLI COMITI CAESS NOSTR. Hercules
standing facing, head l., holding branch in r.
hand, and club and lion-skin in l., mint-
mark, SMT. N, 5.10 gm. ↑.

1239 Follis Ticinum, AD 308–9

Obv. IMP MAXENTIVS P F AVG CONS. Bust, laureate,
in imperial mantle, l., holding eagle-tipped
sceptre in r. hand.

Rev. CONSERV VRB SVAE. Roma seated facing,
head l., in hexastyle temple, holding globe
in r. hand, and sceptre in l.; mint-mark, PT.
Æ, 6.25 gm. ↑.

The inclusion of Maxentius' first consulship in the
obverse inscription dates the issue to this year.

1240 Aureus Aquileia, AD 305–6

Obv. CONSTANTIVS P F AVG. Head, laureate, r.

Rev. CONCORDIA AVGG NOSTR. Concordia seated
l., holding patera and cornucopiae; mint-
mark, AQ. N, 5.03 gm. ↑.

1241 Follis Aquileia, AD 306–7

Obv. IMP C SEVERVS P F AVG. Bust, in laureate
helmet, cuirassed l., holding spear and shield.

Rev. VIRTVS AVGG ET CAESS NN. Severus riding r.,
with shield on l. arm, spearing kneeling
foeman; second foeman prostrate below
horse; mint-mark, AQS. Æ, 8.70 gm. ↓.

1242 Aureus Rome, AD 305–6

Obv. MAXIMIANVS P F AVG. Head of Galerius, laureate, r.
Rev. IOVI CONSERVAT AVGG ET CAESS. Jupiter seated l., holding thunderbolt and sceptre; mint-mark, PR. A͞, 5.20 gm. ↑.

1243 Aureus Rome, AD 306–7

Obv. MAXIMIANVS SEN P F AVG. Head, laureate, r.
Rev. FELIX INGRESS SEN AVG. Roma seated l. on shield, holding shield inscribed
VOT / XXX in r. hand, and sceptre in l.; mint-mark, E|.
  PR
A͞, 5.24 gm. ↑.
The reverse records the return to Rome of Maximian when he became an active Augustus again, when his son, Maxentius, revolted in AD 306.

1244 Aureus Rome, AD 306–7

Obv. D N MAXENTIVS PRINC. Head, laureate, r.
Rev. HERCVLI COMITI AVGG ET CAESS NN. Hercules standing facing, head l., resting r. hand on club, and holding lion-skin and bow in l.; on back, quiver; mint-mark, E|.
  PR
A͞, 5.43 gm. ↑.
In the early coinage after his revolt Maxentius, hoping for recognition from the Senior Augustus, Galerius, adopted the neutral title Princeps and not that of Augustus.

1245 Aureus Rome, AD 307

Obv. CONSTANTINVS NOB C. Head, laureate, r.
Rev. PRINCIPI IVVENTVT. Constantine standing facing, head l., holding standard in r. hand, and sceptre in l.; mint-mark, PR.
A͞, 4.71 gm. ↑.
Maxentius initially coined not only for his father, Maximian, but also for Constantine who was his brother-in-law.

1246 Medallion Rome, AD 308

Obv. IMP C M VAL MAXENTIVS P F AVG. Head, bare, l.
Rev. PRINCIPI IMPERII ROMANI. Mars advancing r., holding spear in r. hand, and shield in l., with trophy over shoulder; mint-mark, PR.
A͞, 21.44 gm. ↑.

1247 Follis Rome, AD 310

Obv. IMP C MAXENTIVS P F AVG. Head, laureate, r.
Rev. FEL PROCESS CONS III AVG N. Maxentius standing facing, head l., r. hand raised in facing quadriga; mint-mark, RET.
Æ, 7.26 gm. ↓.
The reverse depicts the procession for Maxentius' assumption of his third consulship in this year.

1248 Follis Rome, AD 310–11

Obv. IMP MAXENTIVS DIVO ROMVLO N V FILIO. Head of Romulus, bare, r.
Rev. AETERNAE MEMORIAE. Domed tetrastyle shrine with doors; between columns l. and r., statue; above, eagle; mint-mark, REP. Æ, 7.05 gm. ↑.

Memorial coinage for Maxentius' son Romulus, who died in AD 309, and was consecrated. N V = *nobilissimus vir*.

1249 Aureus Carthage, AD 306

Obv. MAXIMINVS NOB C. Head, laureate, r.
Rev. ROMA AETERNA. Roma seated l. on shield, holding Victory on globe and sceptre; mint-mark, PK. N, 5.44 gm. ↓.

Maxentius' early coinage from Carthage still extended recognition to the eastern rulers.

1250 Follis Carthage, AD 306

Obv. M AVR MAXENTIVS NOB CAES. Head, laureate, r.
Rev. SALVIS AVGG ET CAESS FEL KART. Carthage standing facing, head l., holding fruits in both hands; mint-mark, H|.
⎯
Δ

Æ, 8.22 gm. ↓.

The early coinage at Carthage after Maxentius' revolt accords him only the junior title, Caesar.

1251 Follis Carthage, AD 306–7

Obv. MAXENTIVS PRINC INVICT. Head, laureate, r.
Rev. CONSERVATOR AFRICAE SVAE. Africa standing facing, head l., in elephant-skin head-dress, holding standard in r. hand, and tusk in l.; at foot l., lion with captured bull; mint-mark, H|ER.
⎯
B

Æ, 10.63 gm. ↑.

Maxentius title was altered in the next issue at Carthage to *Princeps Invictus*, the title used on his first coinage at Rome. HER in the reverse field marks the coinage as that of one of the Herculian dynasty.

1252 Follis Carthage, AD 308

Obv. IMP ALEXANDER P F AVG. Head, laureate, r.
Rev. ROMAE AETERNAE. Alexander, helmeted, standing facing, head l., holding Victory on globe, and sceptre; mint-mark, PK. Æ, 5.79 gm. ↓.

Carthage was lost to Maxentius when Domitius Alexander revolted in North Africa, and issued his own coinage there.

1253 Aureus Ostia, AD 308–12

Obv. MAXENTIVS P F AVG. Bust, head bare, draped, facing.
Rev. TEMPORVM FELICITAS AVG N. Wolf and twins, r.; mint-mark, POST. N, 5.55 gm. ↑.

The mint organisation from Carthage was used by Maxentius to set up a new mint at Ostia.

1254 Argenteus Ostia, AD 308–12

Obv. MAXENTIVS P F AVG. Head, laureate, r.
Rev. MARTI PROPAG IMP AVG N. Mars standing r.,
 holding sceptre in l. hand, and extending r.
 to female figure; between them, wolf and
 twins, l.; mint-mark, POST Δ. Æ, 3.35 gm. ↑.
Maxentian reverse types frequently allude to the
legends of early Rome, as in this type of Mars, the
father of Romulus and Remus, with Rhea Silvia,
their mother.

1255 Solidus Ostia, AD 312–13

Obv. IMP CONSTANTINVS P F AVG. Head, laureate, r.
Rev. S P Q R OPTIMO PRINCIPI. Legionary eagle
 between two standards; mint-mark, POST.
 N, 4.11 gm. ↑.
Ostia came under the control of Constantine after
his defeat of Maxentius at the Milvian Bridge in
AD 312.

1256 Quarter-follis Siscia, AD 315–16

Obv. GAL VAL MAXIMINVS NOB C. Head, laureate, r.
Rev. GENIO POPVLI ROMANI. Genius standing l.,
 modius on head, chlamys over l. shoulder,
 holding patera in r. hand, and cornucopiae
 in l.; mint-mark, SIS. Æ, 2.78 gm. ↑.
An example of this rarely issued fraction.

1257 Aureus Siscia, AD 306–7

Obv. SEVERVS P F AVG. Head, laureate, r.
Rev. VIRTVS AVGG ET CAESS. Severus advancing r.,
 trophy over shoulder, and dragging captive;
 to r., seated captive; mint-mark, SIS.
 N, 5.38 gm. ↓.

1258 Aureus Siscia, AD 308–11

Obv. GAL VALERIA AVG. Bust with stephane,
 draped, r., on crescent.
Rev. VENERI VICTRICI. Venus standing facing, head
 l., holding up apple in r. hand, and drawing
 drapery over shoulder with l.; mint-mark,
 SIS. N, 4.91 gm. ↓.
Venus Victrix, one of the standard reverses for
imperial ladies, was used on the coinage of Galeria
Valeria, the wife of Galerius.

1259 Follis Siscia, AD 310–11

Obv. GAL VALERIA AVG. Bust with stephane,
 draped, r.
Rev. As on No. 1258; mint-mark, ∪|Γ
 ‾‾‾‾
 SIS
 Æ, 6.76 gm. ↓.

1260 **Follis** Siscia, AD 313

Obv. IMP LICINVS P F AVG. Bust, laureate, draped,
 cuirassed, r.
Rev. IOVI CONSERVATORI AVGG NN. Jupiter
 standing r., holding Victory on globe,
 and sceptre; at foot l., eagle;
 mint-mark, |∈ .
 ‾‾‾
 SIS
 Æ, 3.98 gm. ↓.

1261 **Aureus** Serdica, AD 306–7

Obv. MAXIMINVS NOB C. Head, laureate, r.
Rev. PRINCIPI IVVENTVTIS. Maximinus standing
 l., holding globe and sceptre; to r.,
 two standards; mint-mark, ʒ| .
 ‾‾‾‾
 ·SM·SD
 Aʋ, 5.48 gm. ↑.
A late instance of the numeral ʒ indicating the
standard of 60 aurei to the pound of gold.

1262 **Argenteus** Serdica, AD 306–7

Obv. SEVERVS AVG. Head, laureate, r.
Rev. VIRTVS MILITVM. Gateway with door, and
 three turrets; mint-mark, ·SM·SDA· .
 Æ, 3.16 gm. ↑.

1263 **Follis** Thessalonica, AD 308

Obv. MAXIMINVS·FIL·AVGG. Head, laureate, r.
Rev. GENIO CAESARIS. Genius, modius on head,
 and chlamys over l. shoulder, standing l.,
 holding patera in r. hand, and cornucopiae
 in l.; mint-mark, ∗|Δ .
 ‾‾‾‾‾
 ·SM·TS·
 Æ, 5.87. gm. ↑.
The title *Filius Augustorum* was accorded to
Maximinus – and Constantine – by Galerius after
the Congress of Carnuntum as a sop to their
disappointed hopes of recognition as Augusti.

1264 **Follis** Heraclea, AD 308–9

Obv. IMP C GAL VAL MAXIMINVS P F AVG. Head,
 laureate, r.
Rev. GENIO IMPERATORIS. Genius as on No. 1262;
 mint-mark, ·HTΓ· . Æ, 7.18 gm. ↑.
The reverse inscription of this coin and of Nos.
1262, 1263 and 1267, present Balkan and eastern
mint variations of the normal *Genio Populi Romani*
form.

1265. **Aureus** Nicomedia, AD 308–9

Obv. MAXIMIANVS AVGVSTVS. Head, laureate, r.
Rev. IOVI CONSERVATORI NΚϤΧϹ. Jupiter standing
 l., holding thunderbolt and sceptre; mint-
 mark, SMN. Aʋ, 5.30 gm. ↓.
The final portion of the reverse inscription consists
of the Nicomedian monogram with a numerical
symbol which still awaits satisfactory explanation.

1266 Aureus Nicomedia, AD 310–11

Obv. MAXIMINVS P F AVG. Bust, laureate, in
    imperial mantle, r., raising r. hand and
    holding sceptre in l.
Rev. CONSVL P P PROCONSVL. Emperor standing
    facing, head l., holding globe and baton;
    mint-mark, SMN. *N*, 5.29 gm. ↓.

1267 Follis Nicomedia, AD 310–11

Obv. IMP C GAL VAL MAXIMINVS P F AVG. Head,
    laureate, r.
Rev. GENIO AVGVSTI C͡MH. Genius as on No. 1263;
    mint-mark, SMNB. Æ, 7.44 gm. ↓.
A further variety of reverse inscription accompany-
ing the Genius type cf. Nos. 1263–4, and 1272.

1268 Follis Cyzicus, AD 308

Obv. As No. 1267.
Rev. VIRTVS MILITVM. Gate with doorway, and
    four turrets; mint-mark, MKΓ. Æ, 7.61 gm. ↓.
This type is rarely used as a follis reverse, though it is
one of the standard reverses on silver.

1269 Follis Cyzicus, AD 312–13

Obv. IMP C VAL LICIN LICINIVS P F AVG. Head,
    laureate, r.
Rev. GENIO AVGVSTI C͡MH. Genius as on No. 1263;
    mint-mark, ⎤B.
    ___
    SMK
    Æ, 2.38 gm. ↓.
The significance of the formula C͡MH in the reverse
inscription still remains to be determined.

1270 Aureus Antioch, AD 305

Obv. D N DIOCLETIANO FELICISSIMO SEN AVG. Bust,
    laureate, in imperial mantle, r., holding
    branch and mappa.
Rev. PROVIDENTIA DEORVM QVIES AVGG standing l.,
    holding branch and sceptre; mint-mark,
    ⌣SMAϨ ✳. *N*, 5.37 gm. ↑.
Similar types are used on follis coinage for
Diocletian and Maximian as emperors in retirement
(cf. No. 1226), but this example of Diocletian in
gold is unique.

1271 Follis Antioch, AD 306

Obv. IMP C GAL VAL SEVERVS P F AVG. Head,
    laureate, r.
Rev. GENIO POPVLI ROMANI. Genius standing
    l., modius on head, holding patera in r.
    hand, and cornucopiae in l.; mint-mark,
    ⎤Γ.
    ___
    ANT:
    Æ, 10.26 gm. ↓.
An extremely rare example of the follis coinage at
Antioch for Severus as Augustus.

1272 Follis Antioch, AD 308

Obv. FL VAL CONSTANTINVS FIL AVG. Head,
    laureate, r.
Rev. GENIO FIL AVGG. Genius standing l., modius
    on head, holding patera in r. hand, and
    cornucopiae in l.; mint-mark, $\dfrac{\left.\begin{array}{c}\text{O}\\ \text{E}\end{array}\right|}{\text{ANT}}$.

    Æ, 6.77 gm. ↑.

For the title *Filius Augustorum* accorded to
Constantine see No. 1263. The title was never used
by Constantine himself on coins issued by mints
under his control. For other varieties of Genius
inscription see Nos. 1263, 1264 and 1267.

1273 Follis Antioch, AD 310

Obv. MAXIMINVS NOB CAES. Bust, laureate, half-
    length, in imperial mantle, r., r. hand raised.
Rev. IOVIO PROPAGAT ORBIS TERRARVM.
    Maximinus, togate, standing r., holding
    Victory on globe; to r., altar;
    mint-mark, $\dfrac{\text{A}\left|*\right.}{\text{ANT}}$.

    Æ, 6.51 gm. ↑.

Maximinus is described in the reverse inscription as
Iovius, an unusual identification on coinage of one
of the two Tetrarchic dynasties.

1274 Follis Antioch, AD 310

Obv. MAXIMINVS NOB CAES. Bust, helmeted,
    cuirassed, l., with spear and shield.
Rev. SOLI INVICTO. Sol, radiate, standing
    facing, head l., r. hand raised, in facing
    quadriga; mint-mark, $\dfrac{\text{B}}{\text{ANT}}$.
    Æ, 7.12 gm. ↑.

1275 Follis Alexandria, AD 305–6

Obv. GAL VAL MAXIMINVS NOB CAES. Head,
    laureate, r.
Rev. CONCORD IMPERII. Concordia standing
    facing, head l., holding sceptre in r.
    hand; mint-mark, $\dfrac{\text{S}\left|\begin{array}{c}\text{Δ}\\ \text{P}\end{array}\right.}{\text{ALE}}$.

    Æ, 9.71 gm. ↓.

1276 Aureus Alexandria, AD 306–7

Obv. SEVERVS AVGVST. Head, laureate, r.
Rev. CONCORDIA AVG ET CAES. Concordia
    standing l., holding patera and sceptre;
    mint-mark, $\dfrac{\text{B}\left|\right.}{\text{ALE}}$.
    Æ, 5.36 gm. ↑.

The mention of only one Augustus and one Caesar
in the reverse inscription is unusual on Tetrarchic
coinage. As the Caesar is Maximinus who
controlled this mint and the Augustus is clearly
Severus, Augustus in the West, there is a hint of
some unsuspected political alignment.

1277 Aureus Alexandria, AD 308

Obv. MAXIMINVS NOB CAES. Head, laureate, r.
Rev. SOLE INVICTO. Sol, radiate, standing
    l., raising r. hand, and holding head of
    Serapis in l.; $\underset{\text{ALE}}{\Delta|}$.

    $\mathcal{N}$, 5.47 gm. ↑.

1278 Follis Alexandria, AD 311–13

Obv. IMP C GALER VAL MAXIMINVS P F AVG. Head,
    laureate, r.
Rev. BONO GENIO PII IMPERATORIS. Genius
    standing l., modius on head, holding
    patera in r. hand, and cornucopiae in l.;
    mint-mark, $\underset{\underset{\text{ALE}}{K|X}}{\cup|B}$.

    Æ, 6.99 gm. ↑.

The reverse presents another variety of Genius
inscription, peculiar to Alexandria, cf. Nos. 1263–4,
1267 and 1272.

3 Constantine and Licinius, AD 313–337

The death of Maximinus Daza in AD 313 left only the two Augusti, Constantine and Licinius, to share control of the empire. The uneasy partnership was ruptured on two occasions by civil war, the first in AD 314 in which Licinius lost all his European provinces except Thrace, and the second in AD 324 which resulted in the defeat and death of Licinius, leaving Constantine to rule as sole emperor until his death in AD 337. In AD 317 three new Caesars were appointed, Crispus and Constantine II, sons of Constantine, and Licinius' son, Licinius II. Martinian, appointed an Augustus by Licinius on the outbreak of the second civil war in AD 324, did not survive the defeat of Licinius. Crispus and Fausta, Constantine's empress, were put to death in AD 326. In the latter part of his reign Constantine appointed as additional Caesars his sons Constantius II in AD 324, Constans in AD 333, and his nephew Delmatius in AD 335. Another nephew, Hannibalian, was given the title of king of Armenia in AD 336.

A number of changes in the pattern of mint activity took place in this period. In Britain the London mint was closed in AD 325, and in Gaul a new mint was opened at Arles in AD 313, utilising the mint organisation from Ostia which was now closed. In Italy the mint at Ticinum also was closed in AD 326, while at Aquileia the mint was inactive between AD 325 and 335. In the Balkans Serdica issued coins only for the first year of this period, and the mint at Sirmium was active only between AD 320 and 325. A new, increasingly important and prolific mint was established at Constantine's new foundation, Constantinopolis, in AD 326, though the city was not officially dedicated until AD 330.

In the mints under Constantine's control the recently introduced solidus was the principal gold denomination, but the aureus continued to be issued by the mints of Licinius until his death in AD 324. Silver coinage which is somewhat rare in this period is represented by two denominations, the miliarensis struck at a standard of 72 to the pound, with an average weight of 4.51 gm., and the siliqua on a standard of 96 to the pound, with an average weight of 3.41 gm. The argentiferous bronze follis continued to suffer reductions in its weight standard. At the beginning of this period the weight standard of the follis appears to have fallen to 96 to the pound, with an average weight of 3.41 gm., but by AD 330–337 that standard had been halved to 192 to the pound, an average weight of 1.65 gm.

1279 Follis London, AD 320

Obv. IMP CONSTANTINVS AVG. Bust in crested helmet, cuirassed, l., with spear over shoulder.
Rev. VICTORIAE LAETAE PRINC PERP. Two Victories standing facing one another, together holding shield inscribed VOT / PR on altar; mint-mark, PLN. Æ, 3.38 gm. ↓.

The weight standard of the follis had now been reduced to 96 to the pound.

1280 Aureus Trier, AD 315

Obv. CONSTANTINVS P F AVG. Bust, laureate, draped, cuirassed, r.
Rev. VICTORIBVS AVGG NN VOTIS. Victory seated r. by cuirass and shield, inscribing X / XX on shield, supported by Genius; mint-mark, PTR. ᴀⱴ, 5.30 gm. ↓.

After the introduction of the solidus as the regular gold unit the aureus continued to be struck to mark a special occasion. In this instance the occasion was the celebration of Constantine's decennalia, at the beginning of his tenth regnal year, in July, AD 315.

1281 Follis Trier, AD 321

Obv. CONSTANTINVS IVN NOB C. Bust, laureate, draped, l., holding Victory on globe in r. hand, and mappa in l.
Rev. BEATA TRANQVILLITAS. Globe set on altar inscribed VOT / IS / XX; above, three stars; mint-mark, STR. Æ, 3.27 gm. ↓.

The obverse shows Constantine II as consul, an office held by him jointly with his brother Crispus in AD 321. The *vota* recorded on the obverse are those of Constantine I's quindecennalia.

1282 Follis Trier, AD 323–4

Obv. CONSTANTINVS AVG. Head, laureate, r.
Rev. SARMATIA DEVICTA. Victory advancing r., carrying trophy and palm; at foot, r., seated captive; mint-mark, STR ◡. Æ, 3.46 gm. ↓.

The reverse commemorates the recent defeat by Constantine of a Sarmatian invasion of eastern Pannonia.

1283 Medallion Trier, AD 324

Obv. FL IVL CRISPVS NOB CAES. Bust, laureate, and mantled, l., holding eagle-tipped sceptre in r. hand.
Rev. FELIX PROGENIES CONSTANTINI AVG. Crispus and Constantine II facing one another, clasping hands; between them, Fausta facing, placing hand on their shoulders; mint-mark, PTR. N, 8.68 gm. ↓.

This double-solidus is dated to AD 324 by the consular obverse of Crispus, consul for the third

time in this year. Despite the presence of Fausta, who was not the mother of Crispus, the two Caesars must be Crispus and Constantine II, rather than Constantine II and Constantius II, who became Caesar only in November of this year.

1284 Medallion Trier, AD 324

Obv. FLAVIA MAXIMA FAVSTA AVGVSTA. Bust, head bare, mantled, r.
Rev. PIETAS AVGVSTAE. Fausta, nimbate, seated facing on throne set on platform, holding child on lap; to l., Felicitas, holding caduceus; to r., Pietas; on either side of platform, Genius with wreath; mint-mark, PTR. N, 8.78 gm. ↓.

This double solidus is dated to AD 324 both by Fausta's title Augusta, and its association as a dynastic type with No. 1283. The child on Fausta's lap may be her youngest son, Constans.

1285 Solidus Trier, AD 326

Obv. FL IVL CONSTANTIVS NOB CAES. Head, laureate, r.
Rev. PRINCIPI IVVENTVTIS. Constantius II standing r., holding spear and globe; mint-mark PTR. N, 4.47 gm. ↓.

The traditional reverse for an imperial heir is used for Constantius II who became Caesar in AD 324.

1286 Medallion Trier, AD 332–3

Obv. FL CL CONSTANTINVS IVN NOB CAES. Bust,
laureate, draped, cuirassed, r.
Rev. PRINCIPIA IVVENTVTIS. Constantine II
standing l., holding globe and spear, and
placing foot on supplicant; in ex., SARMATIA;
mint-mark, TR. *N*, 19.70 gm. ↓.
In the campaigns against invading barbarian tribes
the nominal command was vested in Constantine II.

1287 Follis Lyons, AD 314–15

Obv. IMP CONSTANTINVS AVG. Bust, laureate,
draped, cuirassed, r.
Rev. VIRT CONSTANTINI AVG. Constantine
standing l., holding Victory on globe
in r. hand, and spear in l.; to l.,
seated captive; to r., shield; mint-mark,
T|F .
PLG
Æ, 3.83 gm. ↑.

1288 Follis Lyons, AD 321

Obv. CONSTANTINVS AVG. Head, laureate, r.
Rev. VIRTVS EXERCIT. Standard inscribed
VOT / XX; to l. and r., a seated captive;
mint-mark, C|R .
PLG
Æ, 3.25 gm. ↑.

1289 Follis Arles, AD 313–15

Obv. IMP CONSTANTINVS P F AVG. Bust, laureate,
mantled, l., holding eagle-tipped sceptre in
r. hand.
Rev. PROVIDENTIAE AVGG. Female figure standing
r. on prow, received by turreted figure,
standing l., holding sceptre; mint-mark,
PARL. Æ, 3.06 gm. ↓.
Constantine, shown in consular dress, was consul
for the third time in AD 313 when the mint at Ostia
was closed and its organisation moved to Arles,
depicted on the reverse as a turreted figure.

1290 Follis Arles, AD 313–15

Obv. IMP CONSTANTINVS P F AVG. Bust, laureate,
mantled, r., holding eagle-tipped sceptre in
r. hand, and globe in l.
Rev. VTILITAS PVBLICA. Moneta standing l. on
prow, holding scales and cornucopiae,
escorted by soldier, standing l., holding
Victory on globe; mint-mark, PARL.
Æ, 3.14 gm. ↓.
Another type with reference to the opening of the
new mint at Arles.

1291 Follis Rome, AD 317–18

Obv. DIVO MAXIMIANO SEN FORT IMP. Head,
　　laureate, veiled, r.
Rev. REQVIES OPTIMOR MERIT. Maximian seated l.
　　on curule chair, raising r. hand, and holding
　　sceptre in l.; mint-mark, RP. Æ, 2.75 gm. ↓.
The series of consecration or memorial coins issued
by Constantine included his father-in-law,
Maximian, as here, and also his father Constantius
Chlorus, and Claudius Gothicus, claimed as the
founder of the dynasty.

1292 Follis Rome, AD 324–5

Obv. CONSTANTINVS AVG. Head, laureate, r.
Rev. PROVIDENTIAE AVGG. Camp-gate with
　　doorway and two turrets; above, star; mint-
　　mark, RP. Æ, 2.91 gm. ↑.

1293 Medallion Rome, AD 330–7

Obv. VRBS ROMA. Bust, helmeted, draped,
　　cuirassed, l.
Rev. She-wolf to r. in cave, suckling Romulus
　　and Remus; above, two stars; to l. and r., a
　　shepherd, holding a crook. Æ, 25.12 gm. ↑.
The follis coinage honouring Urbs Roma and
issued in AD 330–7 has some medallic parallels
datable to this period.

1294 Medallion Ticinum, AD 315

Obv. IMP CONSTANTINVS MAX P F AVG. Bust,
　　laureate, helmeted, cuirassed, r.
Rev. VICTORIAE LAETAE AVGG NN. Two Victories
　　standing l. and r., holding palm-branch,
　　together holding shield inscribed VOT / X on
　　column inscribed VOT / XX; mint-mark, SMT.
　　N, 8.56 gm. ↓.
This double solidus is part of the coinage
commemorating the celebration of Constantine's
decennial year starting in the course of AD 315.

1295 Solidus Ticinum, AD 316

Obv. COMIS CONSTANTINI AVG. Jugate busts l. of
　　Sol radiate, and Constantine, laureate,
　　draped, cuirassed, raising r. hand, and
　　holding globe in l.
Rev. LIBERALITAS XI IMP IIII COS P PP. Liberalitas
　　standing l., holding abacus and cornucopiae,
　　mint-mark, SMT. N, 4.48 gm. ↓.
Sol, who features on the reverse of an extensive
series of folles, here shares the obverse with the
emperor. The imperial largesse, commonly
recorded on earlier imperial coinage, finds only rare
mention on the later coinage. Note the unusual
placing of the numerals before ĪMP and COS.

1296 Solidus Aquileia, AD 318–19

Obv. CONSTANTINVS P F AVG. Head, laureate, r.
Rev. ADVENTVS AVGVSTI N. Constantine riding l.,
  raising r. hand, and holding spear in l.;
  mint-mark, AQ. *N*, 4.50 gm. ↓.

The reverse shows Constantine's arrival in Aquileia
where his court was established for almost a year.

1297 Medallion Aquileia, AD 319

Obv. LICINIVS IVN NOB CAES. Half-length bust,
  laureate, draped, cuirassed, r., holding
  Victory on globe in l. hand, and spear in r.
Rev. FELICIA. Four children with the attributes of
  the four seasons; in ex., TEMPORA; mint-
  mark, MAQ. *N*, 20.01 gm. ↓.

This four-and-a-half solidus was most probably
issued in honour of young Licinius' first consulship
in this year.

1298 Solidus Aquileia, AD 320

Obv. FL IVL CRISPVS NOB C. Bust, laureate, nude, l.,
  holding spear in r. hand, and shield in l.
Rev. PRINCIPI IVVENTVTIS. Crispus standing r.,
  holding globe and spear; to l. and r., seated
  captive; mint-mark, AQ. *N*, 4.53 gm. ↓.

1299 Miliarensis Aquileia, AD 320

Obv. FL IVL CRISPVS NOB C. Bust, radiate, mantled,
  l., raising r. hand, and holding globe in l.
Rev. VOTA ORBIS ET VRBIS SEN ET P R. Cippus
  inscribed XX / XXX / MVL / FEL set on
  square base; fire on top of cippus;
  mint-mark, L⌐|.
            AQ
  AR, 5.04 gm. ↓.

The denomination of this coin is debatable. If the
letter L in the field is a numeral marking the number
of pieces to the pound, the theoretical weight would
be 6.54 gm.

1300 Medallion Siscia, AD 317

Obv. IMP CONSTANTINVS P F AVG. Bust, radiate,
  draped, cuirassed, r.
Rev. CRISPVS ET CONSTANTINVS IVN NOBB CAESS.
  Confronted busts of Crispus and
  Constantine II, laureate, draped, cuirassed;
  mint-mark, SIS. *N*, 6.61 gm. ↑.

A one-and-a-half solidus commemorating the
elevation of Constantine's sons, Crispus and
Constantine to the rank of Caesar in this year.

1301 Follis Siscia, AD 326-7

Obv. FL HELENA AVGVSTA. Bust, diademed, mantled, r.
Rev. SECVRITAS REIPVBLICE. Securitas standing l., holding branch in r. hand, and raising robe with l.; mint-mark, ·ΓSIS·. Æ, 3.65 gm. ↓.

Helena, mother of Constantine I, was given the titles of Nobilissima Femina and Augusta in AD 324. In the reverse inscription REIPVBLICE shows the alternative and less common ending E for AE (cf. also No. 1305).

1302 Medallion Siscia, AD 326-7

Obv. Head, diademed, looking upwards, r.
Rev. GLORIA CONSTANTINI AVG. Constantine I advancing r., holding trophy over shoulder in l. hand, and dragging captive with r.; at foot, r., seated captive; mint-mark, SIS. AV, 6.80 gm. ↓.

On this one-and-a-half solidus the heavenward-gazing portrait of Constantine I recalls portraits of the divinely inspired Hellenistic rulers.

1303 Siliqua Siscia, AD 334

Obv. FL CONSTANTIS BEA C. Bust, laureate, draped, cuirassed, r.
Rev. VICTORIA CAESARVM. Victory advancing l., holding wreath and palm; mint-mark, SIS. AR, 3.75 gm. ↑.

In the obverse inscription Constans' name is unusually expressed in the genitive case, and is accompanied by the epithet *Bea(tissimus)* not very commonly found on the coinage.

1304 Medallion Sirmium, AD 320

Obv. D N CONSTANTINVS IVN NOB CAES. Bust, laureate, draped, cuirassed, r.
Rev. PRINCIPI IVVENTVTIS. Constantine II standing l., holding standards; mint-mark, SIRM. AV, 6.51 gm. ↑.

The mint of Sirmium was re-opened in AD 320 when it became, for some years, the headquarters of Constantine I.

1305 Solidus Sirmium, AD 324-5

Obv. FL HELENA AVGVSTA. Bust, diademed, mantled, r.
Rev. SECVRITAS REIPVBLICE. Securitas standing l., holding branch in r. hand, and raising robe with l.; mint-mark, SIRM. AV, 4.61 gm. ↑.
Cf. also No. 1301.

1306 Follis Thessalonica, AD 319

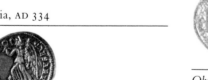

Obv. CONSTANTINVS IVN NOB C. Bust, laureate, cuirassed, r.
Rev. VIRT EXERC. Bird's eye view of a monumental stepped base, surmounted by Sol standing l., raising r. hand, and holding globe in l.; mint-mark, ·TS·B·. Æ, 3.15 gm. ↓.

The traditional description of this reverse type as the plan of a Roman camp is unconvincing, but the proper description and significance of the type remain uncertain.

1307 Medallion Thessalonica, AD 326

Obv. D N CONSTANTINVS MAX AVG. Bust, laureate, mantled, r., holding eagle-tipped sceptre in r. hand, and globe in l.

Rev. SENATVS. Constantine I standing l., holding globe in r. hand, and sceptre in l.; mint-mark, SMTS. N, 13.23 gm. ↓.

The seventh consulship of Constantine I is celebrated by this three-solidus medallion with an unusually elaborate consular obverse and the emperor depicted as a standing figure in consular dress on the reverse also.

1308 Follis Heraclea, AD 325–6

Obv. FLAV MAX FAVSTA AVG. Bust, bare-headed, mantled, r.

Rev. SPES REIPVBLICE. Spes standing front, head l., holding two children in her arms; mint-mark, SMHA. Æ, 3.26 gm. ↑.

The reverse type, if it is intended to show Fausta and two of her sons, is symbolic rather than realistic, as even the youngest, Constans, was by this time four years old.

1309 Follis Constantinople, AD 327

Obv. CONSTANTINVS MAX AVG. Head, laureate, r.

Rev. SPES PVBLIC. Labarum, with three medallions on drapery, and surmounted by Christogram, pierces a serpent; mint-mark,

$$\frac{\text{A}|}{\text{CONS}}.$$

Æ, 2.96 gm. ↓.

Though Constantine's new capital at Constantinople was not dedicated until AD 330, the mint had begun to strike in about AD 326. This is one of the relatively few Constantinian types to include a Christian symbol. The serpent pierced by the labarum must represent the recently defeated Licinius.

1310 Follis Constantinople, AD 328

Obv. CONSTANTINVS MAX AVG. Head, rosette-diademed, r.

Rev. CONSTANTINIANA DAFNE. Victory seated l., head r., holding palm-branch in either hand; to l., trophy and seated captive; mint-mark, $\frac{\varDelta|}{\text{CONS}}$.

Æ, 2.47 gm. ↑.

The reverse refers to the fortress Dafne on the Danube, one of a line of fortifications constructed by Constantine in AD 328.

1311 Follis Constantinople, AD 330–3

Obv. CONSTANTINOPOLI. Constantinopolis, laureate, helmeted, draped, l., with sceptre over l. shoulder.

Rev. Victory standing l. on prow, holding sceptre and shield; mint-mark, CONSIA.

Æ, 2.58 gm. ↓.

A new, reduced, follis coinage begun in AD 330 included a special type honouring the new city dedicated in this year.

1312 Solidus Constantinople, AD 335

Obv. FL DELMATIVS NOB CAES. Bust, laureate, draped, cuirassed, r.
Rev. DELMATIVS CAESAR. Victory advancing l., holding wreath and palm, mint-mark, CONS. *N*, 4.17 gm. ↑.

In AD 335 Constantine nominated his nephew Delmatius as a Caesar.

1313 Solidus Constantinople, AD 336

Obv. CONSTANTINVS MAX AVG. Bust, rosette-diademed, draped, cuirassed, r.
Rev. VICTORIA CONSTANTINI AVG. Victory seated r. on cuirass, inscribing VOT / XX / XX on shield, supported by Genius; mint-mark, CONS. *N*, 4.43 gm. ↑.

Constantine celebrated his tricennalia in this year. The reverse records the *vota* (suscepta) *xxxx* for a further ten years.

1314 Follis Constantinople, AD 336

Obv. FL ANNIBALLIANO REGI. Bust, head bare, draped, cuirassed, r.
Rev. SECVRITAS PVBLICA. Euphrates seated r. on ground, leaning on sceptre; at side, urn; in background, reed; mint-mark, CONSS. Æ, 1.93 gm. ↓.

Hannibalian, a nephew of Constantine, was nominated by him king of Armenia, and evicted the invading Persians from Armenia in AD 336.

1315 Aureus Nicomedia, AD 321

Obv. LICINIVS AVG OB D V FILII SVI. Bust, head bare, draped, cuirassed, facing.
Rev. IOVI CONS LICINI AVG. Jupiter seated facing on throne set on platform, holding Victory on globe in r. hand, and sceptre in l.; at foot l., eagle with wreath in beak; on platform face, SIC X / SIC XX; mint-mark, SMNЄ. *N*, 5.26 gm. ↓.

The obverse presents an unusual, and not very successful, example of a facing portrait. In the obverse inscription OB D V is to be expanded as *ob diem quinquennalium*, the quinquennalia of Licinius II.

1316 Aureus Nicomedia, AD 321

Obv. D N VAL LICIN LICINIVS NOB C. Bust, head bare, draped, cuirassed, facing.
Rev. IOVI CONSERVATORI CAES. As on No. 1316, but on platform face, SIC V / SIC X; mint-mark, SMNΔ. *N*, 5.26 gm. ↑.

An issue for Licinius II, parallel to that above for his father.

1317 **Follis** Nicomedia, AD 324

Obv. D N M MARTINIANVS P F AVG. Bust, radiate, draped, cuirassed, r.
Rev. IOVI CONSERVATORI. Jupiter standing l., holding Victory on globe, and sceptre; at foot l., eagle with wreath; to r., seated captive; mint-mark,

$$\frac{\text{X} \mid \text{IIΓ}}{\text{SMNB}}.$$

Æ, 2.72 gm. ↑.

On the outbreak of the second war between Licinius and Constantius, Licinius appointed Martinian as his fellow-Augustus, but he did not survive the defeat of Licinius.

1318 **Miliarensis** Nicomedia, AD 324

Obv. D N CRISPVS NOB CAESAR. Bust, laureate, cuirassed, r.
Rev. FELICITAS ROMANORVM. Constantine standing l. under arch between his three sons, each holding sceptre and globe; mint-mark, SMN.
Æ, 4.73 gm. ↑.

1319 **Solidus** Nicomedia, AD 325

Obv. Head, diademed, gazing upwards, r.
Rev. CONSTANTINVS CAESAR. Victory advancing l., with wreath and palm; mint-mark, N.
Aʋ, 4.54 gm. ↓.

On this group of solidi the heads of the Caesars are diademed for the first time and are not accompanied by an obverse inscription.

1320 **Follis** Nicomedia, AD 330

Obv. VRBS ROMA. Bust, helmeted, draped, cuirassed, l.
Rev. She-wolf to l., suckling Romulus and Remus; above two stars; mint-mark, SMNB.
Æ, 2.56 gm. ↑.

The coinage inaugurated in AD 330 to honour Constantinopolis (cf. No. 1312) was accompanied by a coinage in honour of the original capital, Rome.

1321 **Follis** Cyzicus, AD 318

Obv. IMP LICINIVS AVG. Bust, laureate, mantled, l., holding mappa in r. hand, and globe and sceptre in l.
Rev. IOVI CONSERVATORI AVGG. Jupiter standing l., holding Victory on globe, and sceptre; mint-mark,

$$\frac{\text{Ω} \mid \varDelta}{\text{SMK}}.$$

Æ, 3.30 gm. ↑.

The consular bust of Licinius connects this issue with his fifth consulship in AD 318.

1322 **Aureus** Antioch, AD 313

Obv. LICINNIVS P F AVG. Head, laureate, r.
Rev. VOTIS V MVLTIS X. Victory standing r., holding on cippus shield, inscribed VI / CTO / RIA / AVG; mint-mark, SMA϶.
Aʋ, 5.31 gm. ↑.

1323 Follis Antioch, AD 317

Obv. DD NN IOVII LICINII INVICT AVG ET CAES. Busts of Licinius I and Licinius II, laureate, draped, facing one another, together holding trophy with two shields.

Rev. I O M ET VIRTVTI DD NN AVG ET CAES. Jupiter standing l., holding sceptre in l. hand; to r., trophy, at foot of which two seated captives; mint-mark, SMATS; Æ, 4.23 gm. ↑.

The propagandistic nature of this issue is apparent from the unusually elaborate obverse type and the inscriptions of both obverse and reverse. In *R I C* p. 547 the mint-mark was read as SMHTA and the issue attributed in error to Heraclea.

1324 Follis Antioch, AD 330–5

Obv. CONSTANTINVS MAX AVG. Bust, rosette-diademed, draped, cuirassed, r.

Rev. GLORIA EXERCITVS. Two soldiers standing facing each other, holding spear and resting hand on shield; between them, two standards; mint-mark, SMANΓ. Æ, 2.90 gm. ↓.

In the series of reduced folles introduced in AD 330, and including the types honouring Constantinople and Rome this was one of the staple types.

1325 Solidus Antioch, AD 336–7

Obv. FL IVL CONSTANS NOB C. Bust, laureate, draped, cuirassed, r.

Rev. VICTORIA CAESAR NN. Victory advancing l. with trophy and palm; mint-mark,

     * | LXXII .
     SMAN·

N, 4.43 gm. ↓.

This series of solidi at Antioch carries in the field the numeral 72, the standard of solidi to the pound of metal.

1326 Follis Alexandria, AD 335–7

Obv. FL IVL CONSTANS NOB C. Bust, laureate, cuirassed, r.

Rev. GLORIA EXERCITVS. As No. 1324, but only one standard, mint-mark, SMALΔ. Æ, 1.70 gm. ↓.

The change in type from two standards to one standard is accompanied by a further reduction in the weight of the follis.

4 The three sons of Constantine I, AD 337–340

The death of Constantine in May AD 337 was followed in September by the elimination of his two nephews, Dalmatius and Hannibalian, and the proclamation as Augusti of his three sons, Constantine II, Constantius II and Constans, between whom the empire was divided. Britain, Gaul and Spain fell to Constantine, Africa, Italy Illyricum and Thrace to Constans, and the remaining eastern provinces to Constantius. In AD 360, however, in an abortive invasion of Italy Constantine was killed, and control of his provinces passed to Constans.

In this short joint reign no changes took place in the mints active in the latter part of Constantine I's reign, and the monetary system of that period continued unchanged, except for the introduction of the large silver denomination of 4 siliquae of an average weight 12.65 gm.

1327 Solidus Trier, AD 337–40

Obv. FL CL CONSTANTINVS AVG. Bust in laureate-rosetted diadem, draped, cuirassed, r.
Rev. VIRTVS EXERCITVS GALL. Mars advancing r., with spear and trophy; at foot l. and r., seated captive; mint-mark, TR. N, 4.16 gm. ↓.

1328 Miliarensis Trier, AD 337–40

Obv. CONSTANTINVS AVG. As No. 1327.
Rev. CONSTANTINVS AVG. Four standards; mint-mark, SMTR. Æ, 3.68 gm. ↓.

1329 Siliqua Trier, AD 337–40

Obv. FL IVL CONSTANTIVS AVG. Bust, laureate, draped, cuirassed, r.
Rev. PAX AVGVSTORVM. Constantius II standing l., holding labarum marked with Chi-Rho; mint-mark, TRS. Æ, 3.36 gm. ↓.

In the mints of one of the Augusti, coinage was struck in the name of the other two brothers also.

1330 Medallion Rome, AD 337–40

Obv. VICT CONSTANTINVS AVG. Bust, laureate, draped, cuirassed, r.
Rev. VICTORI GENTIVM, and in ex., BARBARR. Constantine II galloping r., levelling spear at barbarian; below horse, prostrate barbarian; no mint-mark. Æ, 36.94 gm. ↑.

1331 Medallion Aquileia, AD 337–40

Obv. CONSTANTIVS P F AVG. Bust in laureate-
rosetted diadem, draped, cuirassed, r.
Rev. VIRTVS CONSTANTI AVG. Constantius II
standing l., holding Chi-Rho labarum in r.
hand, and sceptre in l.; at foot r., seated
captive; mint-mark, *SMAQ. *N*, 6.51 gm. ↑.
The reverse of this 1½ solidus medallion alludes to
the war with Persia which engaged Constantius'
attention from the beginning of his reign.

1332 Solidus Siscia, AD 337

Obv. CONSTANTINVS P F AVG. Bust in laureate-
rosetted diadem, draped, cuirassed, r.
Rev. GAVDIVM POPVLI ROMANI. Wreath enclosing
SIC / XX / SIC XXX; mint-mark, SIS*.
N, 3.90 gm. ↑.
The vota celebrated on the reverse are those for the
vicennalia of Constantine II, appointed Caesar in
AD 317.

1333 Siliqua Siscia, AD 337–40

Obv. CONSTANTIVS P F AVG. Bust in laureate-
rosetted diadem, draped, cuirassed, r.
Rev. CONSTANTIVS AVG. Three palm branches;
above, a star; mint-mark, ·SIS·.
R, 3.15 gm. ↑.

1334 Medallion Siscia, AD 337

Obv. AVGVSTVS. Head in laureate-rosetted diadem, r.
Rev. CAESAR. within a wreath; mint-mark, SIS.
R, 12.66 gm. ↑.
The attribution and date of this 4 siliquae piece is a
matter of controversy. It has been attributed to
Constantine I and to the last year of his reign, but,
as the portrait does not particularly resemble
Constantine I, and since known examples of this
denomination are in the names of Constantius II and
Constans as Augusti (cf. Nos. 1357, 1359), the
portrait is probably more correctly to be identified
as that of Constantine II.

1335 Medallion Thessalonica, AD 337–40

Obv. FL IVL CONSTANS PIVS FELIX AVG. Bust in laureate-rosetted diadem, draped, cuirassed, r.

Rev. SALVS ET SPES REIPVBLICAE. The three sons of Constantine standing, holding spear in r. hand, and resting l. hand on shield, mintmark, TES. N, 19.25 gm. ↓.

The three Augusti who succeeded in AD 337 are described as representing the salvation and hope of the state. The central figure, shown facing, is presumably the eldest brother Constantine II to whom the flanking figures of Constantius II and Constans turn their heads.

1336 Solidus Thessalonica, AD 337–8

Obv. FL IVL CONSTANS P F AVG. Bust in laureate-rosetted diadem, draped, cuirassed, r.

Rev. GAVDIVM POPVLI ROMANI. Wreath enclosing VOT / V / MVLT / X; mint-mark, TSЄ. N, 4.49 gm. ↓.

Constans, appointed Caesar in AD 333, celebrated his quinquennalia in this year.

1337 Medallion Thessalonica, AD 337–40

Obv. As No. 1336.

Rev. VIRTVS EXERCITVM. Constans standing l., holding trophy in r. hand, and resting l. on shield; at foot l. and r., seated captive; mintmark, TES. N, 6.70 gm. ↓.

Medallion of 1½ solidi.

1338 Siliqua Constantinople, AD 337–40

Obv. Head, laureate, r.

Rev. CONSTANTIVS AVGVSTVS. Victory advancing l., with wreath and palm; mint-mark, C·Γ. R, 2.97 gm. ↑.

1339 Follis Constantinople, AD 337

Obv. DV CONSTANTINVS P T AVGG. Head, veiled, r.

Rev. Constantine in quadriga, r.; above, hand descending from heaven; mint-mark, CONS. Æ, 1.39 gm. ↑. (See also Nos. 1362 and 1363.)

Constantine, though baptised on his death-bed, was portrayed as deified on coinage after his death, the last emperor to be consecrated.

1340 Follis Constantinople, AD 337–40

Obv. FL IVL HELENAE AVG. Bust, laureate and
  pearled, draped, r.
Rev. PAX PVBLICA. Pax standing l., holding branch
  and sceptre; mint-mark, CONSЄ.
  Æ, 1.70 gm. ↑.

Coinage in the name of Helena, mother of
Constantine I, continued to be issued in this period,
though she had died in AD 328.

1341 Solidus Antioch, AD 338–9

Obv. FL IVL CONSTANTIVS PERP AVG. Bust in pearl
  diadem, draped, cuirassed, r.
Rev. VICTORIA AVGVSTORVM. Victory seated r. on
  cuirass, inscribing VOT / XV / MVLT / XX on
  shield, supported by Genius, mint-mark,
  SMANA. N, 4.36 gm. ↑.

As Constantius II was appointed Caesar in AD 324,
the vows for his fifteenth year recorded here are of
the year AD 338–9.

5 Constantius II and Constans, AD 340–350

The death of Constantine II in AD 340 left his two brothers Constantius II and Constans as joint Augusti, the control of Constantine's provinces passing to Constans. After only ten years, however, the revolt of Magnentius in Gaul led to the defeat and death of Constans in AD 350. The mints active for the three brothers continued without change in this period. In the monetary system the precious-metal denominations were continued without change, but a new series of silvered bronze or billon denominations was introduced towards the end of the period in AD 348 on the occasion of the eleven hundredth anniversary of Rome's foundation. The names of the denominations remain the subject of controversy, as are the relation of the denominations to each other, and their tariffing in terms of the precious-metal coinage. For convenience, until these questions are satisfactorily resolved, the description of these coins in terms of size, i.e. Æ 2 and Æ 3, is retained in this period. There is some evidence that the larger, the Æ 2, may be the *maiorina* mentioned in fourth-century legislation.

1342 **Solidus** Trier, AD 342–3

Obv. CONSTANS AVGVSTVS. Bust, pearl-diademed, draped, cuirassed, r.
Rev. VICTORIAE DD NN AVGG. Two Victories standing facing one another, holding wreath enclosing VOT / X / MVLT / XX; mint-mark, TR. Ν, 4.51 gm. ↓.
The vota for Constans' decennalia place this issue in AD 346–7.

1343 **Miliarensis** Trier, AD 342–3

Obv. FL IVL CONSTANS P F AVG. Bust in laureate-rosetted diadem, draped, cuirassed, r.
Rev. GAVDIVM ROMANORVM. Labarum inscribed VOT / X / MVLT / XX between two seated captives; mint-mark, TR. Æ, 4.68 gm. ↓.

1344 **Half-siliqua** Trier, AD 347–8

Obv. CONSTANTIVS P F AVG. Bust, pearl-diademed, draped, cuirassed, r.
Rev. VICTORIA DD NN AVGG. Victory advancing l., with wreath and palm; mint-mark, TR. Æ, 1.13 gm. ↓.

1345 **Follis** Trier, AD 347

Obv. CONSTANS P F AVG. Bust in laureate-rosetted diadem, draped, cuirassed, r.
Rev. VICTORIAE DD AVGG Q NN. Two Victories standing facing one another, each holding wreath; mint-mark, leaf / TRP.
Æ, 2.01 gm. ↓.
One of the last issues of this coin denomination before the introduction of the new billon denominations in AD 348.

1346 Billon Trier, AD 348–50

Obv. D N CONSTANS P F AVG. Bust, pearl-diademed, draped, cuirassed, r.
Rev. FEL TEMP REPARATIO. Phoenix standing r. on globe; mint-mark, TRS·. 2.62 gm. ↑.
This represents the smaller of the three denominations of the reformed coinage introduced in AD 348. The reverse inscription *Fel(icium) Temp(orum) Reparatio* is regarded as a reference to Rome's eleven hundredth anniversary in AD 348.

1347 Billon Lyons, AD 348–50

Obv. D N CONSTANS P F AVG. Bust, rosette-diademed, draped, cuirassed, r.
Rev. FEL TEMP REPARATIO. Warrior with shield on l. arm spearing barbarian falling from horse l.; mint-mark, PLG*. 5.05 gm. ↑.
This represents the larger of the two denominations of the billon coinage introduced in AD 348.

1348 Nine-siliquae Arles, AD 340–50

Obv. CONSTANTIVS P F AVG. Bust in laureate-rosetted diadem, draped, cuirassed, r.
Rev. VICTORIA AVGVSTORVM. Victory advancing l. with wreath and palm; in ex., PARL. Ν, 1.69 gm. ↓.
An example of the nine-siliqua piece, an unusual denomination, that is three-eights of the solidus.

1349 Siliqua Rome, AD 347

Obv. FL IVL CONSTANS P F AVG. Bust in laureate-rosetted diadem, draped, cuirassed, r.
Rev. FEL TEMP REPARATIO. Victory standing r., l. foot on globe, inscribing VOT / XX on shield supported on head by figure kneeling r.; mint-mark, R. Æ, 2.85 gm. ↓.

1350 Billon Rome, AD 348–50

Obv. D N CONSTANS P F AVG. Bust in laureate-rosetted diadem, draped, cuirassed, r.; behind head, A.
Rev. FEL TEMP REPARATIO. Emperor standing l. on galley l., holding phoenix on globe in r. hand, and standard with Chi-Rho in l.; on stern, seated Victory steering galley; mint-mark, A| . 5.44 gm. ↓.   RB
Of the larger of the two billon denominations there are two varieties of which this, the heavier, is marked by A behind the obverse bust.

1351 Billon Rome, AD 348–50

Obv. DN CONSTANTIVS P F AVG. Bust, pearl-diademed, draped, cuirassed, l., holding globe in r. hand; behind head, N.
Rev. FEL TEMP REPARATIO. Emperor, nimbate, with shield on l. arm, galloping r., thrusting with spear at two barbarians kneeling before him; mint-mark, N| . 3.69 gm. ↑.   RP
The second and lighter variety of the larger billon denomination is marked by N behind the bust.

1352 Billon Rome, AD 348–50

Obv. As No. 1351.
Rev. FEL TEMP REPARATIO. Helmeted soldier with spear in l. hand, head turned l., dragging small figure from hut beneath tree; mint-mark, |N .
    RS

4.98 gm. ↓.

Another example of the N-marked variety represents another of the reverse types associated with the *Fel Temp Reparatio* inscription.

1353 Medallion Rome, AD 340–7

Obv. CONSTANTINOPOLIS. Bust, helmeted, draped, cuirassed, l., with spear over l. shoulder.
Rev. VICTORIA AVGG NN. Res Publica turreted, seated l., holding branch and cornucopiae, crowned by Victory standing facing, head l., and holding palm-branch. Æ, 38.26 gm. ↑.

The Constantinopolis type, first used to celebrate the foundation of Constantinople in AD 330, continued to be used at various dates in the subsequent decades.

1354 Medallion Rome, AD 340–50

Obv. FL IVL CONSTANS P F AVG. Bust in laureate-rosetted diadem, draped, cuirassed, r.
Rev. ROMA BEATA. Roma, helmeted, seated l., holding Victory on globe in r. hand, and spear in l.; beside her, a shield. Æ, 25.24 gm. ↑.

Types honouring Rome, parallel to those for Constantinople, were also continued in varied form long after the first appearance in AD 330.

1355 Solidus Aquileia, AD 343–4

Obv. CONSTANTIVS AVGVSTVS. Bust in laureate-rosetted diadem, draped, cuirassed, r. (all enclosed by wreath).
Rev. VICTORIAE DD NN AVGG. Victory seated r. on cuirass, holding shield inscribed VOT / XX / MVLT / XXX and supported by Genius; mint-mark, SMAQ; (all enclosed by wreath). N, 4.49 gm. ↓.

The vota on the reverse type are those associated with the vicennalia of Constantius II in this year. At the mints of Trier and Siscia as well as Aquileia, some issues of solidi have obverse and reverse types enclosed by a wreath in place of the usual border of dots.

1356 Miliarensis Aquileia, AD 346–7

Obv. D N CONSTANS P F AVG. Bust in laureate-rosetted diadem, draped, cuirassed, r.

Rev. VICTORIAE DD NN AVGG. Victory seated r. on cuirass, holding shield inscribed VOT / X / MVLT / XX; mint-mark, AQS. Æ, 4.51 gm. ↑.
The decennalia of Constans recorded by the vows on the reverse type fell in AD 343, but the coin is somewhat later.

1357 Medallion Siscia, *c.*AD 343–5

Obv. FL IVL CONSTANTIVS P F AVG. Bust in laureate-rosetted diadem, draped, cuirassed.
Rev. GAVDIVM POPVLI ROMANI. Wreath enclosing SIC / XX / SIC / XXX; mint-mark, ·SIS·. Æ, 13.57 gm. ↑.
An example of the silver multiple of 4 siliquae. The vicennalia vows for Constantius II are recorded by this variety of votive formula.

1358 Follis Siscia, AD 347

Obv. CONSTANTIVS P F AVG. Bust, rosette-diademed, draped, cuirassed, r.
Rev. VICTORIA AVGG. Victory advancing l., with wreath and palm; mint-mark, $\frac{*|}{*ΔSIS*}$.
Æ, 1.37 gm. ↓.
An example of one of the latest issues of this category of coin at Siscia before the introduction of the new system in AD 348.

1359 Medallion Thessalonica, AD 340–50

Obv. FL IVL CONSTANTIVS PIVS FELIX AVG. Bust in laureate-rosetted diadem, draped, cuirassed, r.
Rev. TRIVMFATOR GENTIVM BARBARARVM. Emperor standing l., holding labarum in r. hand, and resting l. on shield; mint-mark, TES. Æ, 12.98 gm. ↓.
On this silver multiple of 4 siliquae the emperor's epithets Pius Felix are recorded in full.

1360 Billon Constantinople, AD 348–50

Obv. D N CONSTANTIVS P F AVG. Bust, pearl-diademed, draped, cuirassed, l., holding globe in r. hand.
Rev. FEL TEMP REPARATIO. Emperor standing l., holding labarum in r. hand, and resting l. on shield; to l., two kneeling captives; mint-mark, $\frac{Γ|}{CONSA*}$.
5.08 gm. ↑.
This variety of *Fel Temp Reparatio* was used more frequently at eastern mints.

1361 Medallion Antioch, AD 346

Obv. CONSTANTIVS AVGVSTVS. Bust, pearl-diademed, mantled, r., holding eagle-tipped sceptre in l. hand, and mappa in r.

Rev. DD NN CONSTANTIVS CONSTANS AVGG. Constantius II and Constans, nimbate, standing facing, in consular dress, holding sceptre in r. hand, and mappa in l.; mint-mark, SMANT. *N*, 6.80 gm. ↑.

A double-solidus issued on the occasion of the joint consulship of Constantius II and Constans in AD 346.

1362 Follis Antioch, AD 342

Obv. DV CONSTANTINVS PT AVGG. Head, veiled, r.

Rev. IVST VEN MEM. Justitia standing l., holding scales and cornucopiae; mint-mark, SMANI. Æ, 1.56 gm. ↑.

Coinage was issued to commemorate the deified Constantine, described as *P(a)t(er) Augustorum*, father of the emperors (cf. No. 1339). The reverse inscription is perhaps to be expanded and construed as *iustus venerandae memoriae*.

1363 Follis Antioch, AD 347

Obv. As No. 1362

Rev. VN MR. Constantine I, veiled, draped, standing r.; mint-mark, SMANε. Æ, 1.58 gm. ↑.

Another type in the commemorative coinage for Constantine I (cf. No. 1362). In the reverse inscription VN MR = *venerandae memoriae*.

6 Constantius II with Gallus and Julian Caesars, AD 350–360

The revolt of Magnentius gave him immediate control of Gaul and very soon of Africa and Italy also, where in Rome Nepotian, a cousin of Constantius, had reigned for a few weeks in June, AD 350. In the Balkans Vetranio, commander of the forces on the Danube, was proclaimed emperor and was temporarily recognised by Constantius. Magnentius, failing to secure recognition from Constantius, advanced into the Balkans but was defeated by Constantius at Mursa, and Vetranio abdicated. By AD 353 Constantius had recovered Italy and Gaul, and Magnentius and his brother had committed suicide. In AD 351 Constantius had created his nephew Constantius Gallus his Caesar and, following his execution in AD 354, appointed his other nephew, Julian, as Caesar. After some years of successful campaigning in Gaul, Julian was proclaimed Augustus by his troops in AD 360.

The events of the period occasioned some changes in mint activity. In Gaul Magnentius set up a new mint at Amiens in AD 350, but this was closed in AD 353 shortly after the reconquest of Gaul by Constantius. Constantius in his passage through Italy against Magnentius opened a new mint at Milan in AD 352–3, and in the Balkans, when Siscia fell briefly into the hands of Magnentius, the mint at Sirmium was re-opened by Constantius.

No changes were made in the precious-metal denominations except that towards the end of his reign Magnentius issued a series of lighter solidi of an average weight of 3.80 gm. Magnentius also initially continued a billon series of the Æ 2 module, though this tended to decline in weight and fineness, and in AD 352 he introduced a new larger Æ 1 coin of an average weight of 9.00 gm., but with a negligible percentage of silver. By about AD 354 the billon coin of Æ 3 module had declined to an average weight of 2.5 gm., and the standard is seen to be further reduced in subsequent issues; it was succeeded towards the end of the period by an ever smaller Æ 4 denomination.

1364 Æ 2 Amiens, AD 350

Obv. D N MAGNENTIVS P F AVG. Bust, head bare, draped, cuirassed, r.; behind head, A.
Rev. GLORIA ROMANORVM. Emperor riding r., thrusting with spear at barbarian kneeling l.; beneath horse, shield and broken spear; mint-mark, AMB ⚹ . 3.96 gm. ↑.

Contrary to normal custom in this period the portrait of Magnentius is usually shown bare-headed. This Æ 2 denomination continues to be marked with A behind bust.

1365 Æ 1 Amiens, AD 353

Obv. As No. 1364, but without A behind bust.
Rev. SALVS DD NN AVG ET CAES. Chi-Rho flanked by alpha and omega; mint-mark, AMB. 8.42 gm. ↑.

This new larger and heavier Æ 1 denomination was introduced by Magnentius towards the end of his reign.

1366 Medallion Trier, AD 350

Obv. IM CAE MAGNENTIVS AVG. Bust, bare-headed, draped, cuirassed, r.

Rev. SECVRITAS REIPVBLICE. Securitas standing facing, head r., placing r. hand on head, and leaning l. elbow on column; mint-mark, TR. Æ, 12.94 gm. ↓.

The silver multiple of four siliquae was issued only very rarely for Magnentius.

1367 Æ 2 Trier, AD 350–1

Obv. As No. 1366.

Rev. FELICITAS REIPVBLICE. Emperor standing l., holding Victory on globe in r. hand, and standard with Chi-Roh in l., mint-mark, ⎵|A .
TRS
Æ, 6.28 gm. ↓.

1368 Solidus Trier, AD 351–3

Obv. D N MAGNENTIVS P F AVG. Bust, bare-headed, draped, cuirassed, r.

Rev. VICTORIA AVG LIB ROMANOR. Victory standing r. and Libertas, holding sceptre, standing l., together holding trophy on shaft; mint-mark, TR. Ꞥ, 3.75 gm. ↓.

1369 Solidus Trier, AD 353

Obv. D N DECENTIVS FORT CAES. Bust, bare-headed, draped, cuirassed, r.

Rev. VICTORIA CAES LIB ROMANOR. As No. 1368. Ꞥ, 3.84 gm. ↓.

Coinage was issued for Decentius, the emperor's brother whom Magnentius appointed Caesar in AD 351. The solidus issued by Magnentius towards the end of the reign was of this lighter weight.

1370 Æ 2 Trier, AD 353

 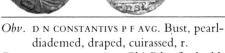

Obv. D N CONSTANTIVS P F AVG. Bust, pearl-diademed, draped, cuirassed, r.

Rev. SALVS AVG NOSTRI. Chi-Rho flanked by alpha and omega; mint-mark, TRS∗. 5.76 gm. ↑.

In a revolt against Magnentius Trier issued for Constantius II a coinage with a version of the Chi-Rho reverse used by Magnentius.

1371 Solidus Trier, AD 354

Obv. D N CONSTANTIVS NOB CAES. Bust of Gallus, bare-headed, draped, cuirassed, r.
Rev. GLORIA REIPVBLICAE. Roma seated, head r., and Constantinopolis seated, head l., foot on prow, together holding wreath enclosing VOT / V / MVLT / X; mint-mark, TR. *N*, 4.41 gm. ↓.

1372 Solidus Lyons, AD 353

Obv. D N MAGNENTIVS AVG. Bust, bare-headed, draped, cuirassed, r.
Rev. VICT AVG LIB ROM ORB. As No. 1368; mint-mark, NLVG. *N*, 4.09 gm. ↓.

1373 Æ 2 Lyons, AD 352

Obv. D N MAGNENTIVS P F AVG. Bust, bare-headed, draped, cuirassed, r.; behind bust, A.
Rev. VICTORIAE DD NN AVG ET CAE. Two Victories standing facing one another, together holding wreath enclosing VOT / V / MVLT / X; mint-mark, SV over RPLG. 5.65 gm. ↑.

1374 Æ 3 Arles, AD 354

Obv. D N CONSTANTIVS P F AVG. Bust, pearl-diademed, draped, cuirassed, r.
Rev. FEL TEMP REPARATIO. Soldier standing l., with shield on l. arm, thrusting with spear at warrior falling from horse and raising arm; below soldier, shield; mint-mark, D over PCON.
3.01 gm. ↑.

Coinage for Constantius II was resumed at Arles after the defeat of Magnentius. The standard billon coin was reduced about this date to the Æ 3 module. Constantius II celebrated his tricennalia in AD 353 at Arles when he honoured the city by regranting the dynastic name, Constantia.

1375 Solidus Arles, AD 355

Obv. FL CL IVLIANVS NOB CAES. Bust, bare-headed, draped, cuirassed, r.
Rev. GLORIA REIPVBLICAE. Roma seated facing and Constantinopolis seated l., foot on prow, together holding wreath inscribed VO / TIS / V; mint-mark, * over KONSTAN.
N, 4.41 gm. ↑.

The anticipatory vota are probably to be associated with Julian's appointment as Caesar.

1376 Æ 2 Rome, AD 350

Obv. IMP CAE MAGNENTIVS AVG. Bust, bare-headed, draped, cuirassed, r.
Rev. VICTORIA AVG LIB ROMANOR. Emperor standing r., holding banner with eagle in r. hand, and branch in l., placing l. foot on captive seated r.; mint-mark, A over R·F·B.
5.22 gm. ↓.

Very soon after his revolt in Gaul Magnentius gained control of Italy and the mint at Rome.

1377 Medallion Rome, AD 350

1379 Medallion Rome, AD 350

Obv. D N CONSTANTIVS P F AVG. Bust, in laureate-rosetted diadem, draped, cuirassed, r.

Rev. LARGITIO. Emperor, diademed, enthroned facing, holding scroll in l. hand, and with feet on footstool; to r., Roma standing facing, head l., placing r. hand on emperor's shoulder, and holding spear in l.; to r., Res Publica, turreted, standing r., bowing to emperor, and holding out robe to receive largesse. Æ, 22.22 gm. ↑.

This medallion in the name of Constantius II was issued by Magnentius in early AD 350 while he still hoped to secure recognition from Constantius.

1378 Medallion Rome, AD 350

Obv. D N CONSTANTIVS P F AVG. Bust in laureate-rosetted diadem, draped, cuirassed, l., raising r. hand.

Rev. VICTORIA AVGVSTORVM. Emperor standing facing, head l., raising r. hand and holding spear; to l., Victory standing l., holding palm-branch in r. hand, and placing l. on emperor's shoulder. Æ, 17.15 gm. ↓.

Another medallion in the same context as No. 1377.

Obv. IMP CAE MAGNENTIVS AVG. Bust, bare-headed, draped, cuirassed, r.

Rev. VICTORIA AVGG. Victory advancing l., with wreath and palm, spurning captive kneeling l., head r. Æ, 17.74 gm. ↑.

A medallion from the same group as Nos. 1377–8, but in the name of Magnentius himself.

1380 Æ 2 Rome, AD 350

Obv. FL POP NEPOTIANVS P F AVG. Bust, bare-headed, draped, cuirassed, r.

Rev. VRBS ROMA. Roma seated l. on shield, holding Victory on globe and spear; mint-mark, RQ. 4.80 gm. ↓.

The usurpation of Nepotian, a cousin of Constantius II, lasted only from 3–30 June AD 350 at Rome.

1381 Solidus Rome, AD 351–2

Obv. MAG DECENTIVS N CS. Bust, bare-headed, draped, cuirassed, r.

Rev. VICTORIA AVG LIB ROMANOR. Victory with palm branch over shoulder standing r., and Libertas, holding sceptre in l. hand, standing l., together holding trophy on staff: mint-mark, RЄ. N, 4.38 gm. ↓.

This example shows evidence of having been overstruck on a solidus of Constantine I.

1382 Medallion Rome, AD 352–4

Obv. D N FL CL CONSTANTIVS NOB CAES. Bust, bare-headed, draped, cuirassed, r.
Rev. VRBS ROMA. Roma seated l. on shield, holding Victory on globe and spear. Æ, 18.76 gm. ↓.

One of a series of medallions probably to be associated with the recovery of Italy from Magnentius, bearing the name of Constantius Gallus.

1383 Solidus Rome, AD 355–7

Obv. DN CL IVLIANVS N C. Bust, bare-headed, draped, cuirassed, r.
Rev. FEL TEMP REPARATIO. Roma seated facing, and Constantinopolis, holding sceptre, seated l., r. foot on prow, together holding wreath enclosing star; mint-mark, ↘RSMS✶. *N*, 4.45 gm. ↑.

1384 Solidus Rome, AD 357

Obv. FL IVL CONSTANTIVS PERP AVG. Bust, pearl-diademed, mantled, l., holding mappa and sceptre.
Rev. FELICITAS ROMANORVM. As No. 1383 but VOT / XXXV / MVLT / XXXX, mint-mark, RSMϵ✶. *N*, 4.44 gm. ↑.

This appears to be the earliest in the series of 'consular' solidi which are a feature of the later fourth- and fifth-century coinage. An issue for Constantius' ninth consulship.

1385 Medallion Rome, AD 355–61

Obv. D N CL IVLIANVS N C. Bust, bare-headed, draped, cuirassed, r.
Rev. VIRTVS AVG N. Emperor standing l., holding branch and standard, and placing r. foot on seated captive. Æ, 14.35 gm. ↓.

1386 Solidus Milan, AD 354

Obv. FL IVL CONSTANTIVS PERP AVG. Bust, pearl-diademed, draped, cuirassed, r.
Rev. GLORIA REIPVBLICAE. Roma seated r. and Constantinopolis holding sceptre, seated l., r. foot on prow, together holding wreath inscribed VOT / XXX / MVLT / XXXX; mint-mark, SMMED. *N*, 4.47 gm. ↑.

A new mint at Milan was opened by Constantius II when he advanced into Italy in AD 352, and this issue commemorating his tricennalia was issued in AD 354.

1387 Solidus Aquileia, AD 350–1

Obv. FL MAGNENTIVS TR P F AVG. Bust, bare-headed, draped, cuirassed, r.
Rev. RESTITVTOR LIBERTATIS. Emperor standing l., holding Victory on globe, and standard with Chi-Rho; mint-mark, SMAQ. *N*, 4.27 gm. ↑.

In the unusual inscription the abbreviation, TR, is to be expanded as *Tr(iumphator)*.

1388 Miliarensis Aquileia, AD 350–1

Obv. D N MAGNENTIVS P F AVG. Bust, bare-headed, draped, cuirassed, r.
Rev. VICTORIAE DD NN AVGG. Victory seated r. on cuirass, holding shield inscribed VOT / V / MVLT / X; mint-mark, *AQ·. Æ, 4.28 gm. ↑.

1389 Solidus Siscia, AD 350

Obv. D N VETRANIO P F AVG. Bust, laureate, draped, cuirassed, r.
Rev. SALVATOR REIPVBLICAE. Emperor standing l., holding standard with Chi-Rho, being crowned by Victory, standing l., holding palm-branch; mint-mark, SIS.
Ν, 4.47 gm. ↓.
On the revolt of Magnentius in the West, Vetranio, commander of the Danube forces, was proclaimed Augustus.

1390 Miliarensis Siscia, AD 350

Obv. As No. 1389.
Rev. GAVDIVM POPVLI ROMANI. Wreath enclosing VOT / V / MVLT / X; mint-mark, ‾‾‾‾‾.
                                                      SIS
Æ, 4.90 gm. ↓.
At the outset of a reign anticipatory vota are frequently recorded on the coinage.

1391 Æ 2 Siscia, AD 350

Obv. As No. 1389.
Rev. HOC SIGNO VICTOR ERIS. Type as No. 1389; mint-mark, A⏐‾‾‾.
                                              ·∈SIS*
7.32 gm. ↓.
The reverse inscription 'In this sign shalt thou conquer' refers to the accompaniment of Constantine the Great's vision of the Christian Cross before the battle of the Milvian Bridge in AD 312.

1392 Miliarensis Sirmium, AD 351–4

Obv. D N CONSTANTIVS NOB CAES. Head, bare, r.
Rev. FELICITAS ROMANORVM. Constantius, diademed, and Constantius Gallus, bare-headed, standing facing, heads turned towards each other, each holding a spear under an arch; mint-mark, *SIRM*.
Æ, 4.37 gm. ↓.
The mint at Sirmium was re-opened by Constantius II in AD 351 when Magnentius briefly controlled the mint at Siscia. This piece is in the name of Gallus.

1393 Æ 2 Thessalonica, AD 350

Obv. D N VETRANIO P F AVG. Bust, pearl-diademed, draped, cuirassed, r.
Rev. CONCORDIA MILITVM. Emperor standing facing, head l., holding in each hand standard with Chi-Rho; mint-mark, A⏐B .
4.53 gm. ↓.   ·TSA·
The Balkan mint of Thessalonica struck for Vetranio during his brief rule as Augustus.

1394 Æ 2 Thessalonica, AD 351–4

Obv. D N CONSTANTIVS NOB CAES. Bust, bare-
headed, draped, cuirassed, r.

Rev. FEL TEMP REPARATIO. Emperor standing
l., holding Victory on globe, and
standard with Chi-Rho; with r. foot he
spurns seated captive; mint-mark, $\frac{\Gamma\,|\,*}{*TS\Delta\cdot}$.
6.34 gm. ↓.

This unusual variety of the *Fel Temp Reparatio* type
appeared on the billon coinage at Thessalonica
when it resumed coinage for Constantius II and his
Caesar.

1395 Solidus Thessalonica, AD 358–9

Obv. D N CONSTANTIVS P F AVG. Head, pearl-
diademed, r.

Rev. GLORIA REIPVBLICAE. Roma seated facing,
head r., and Constantinopolis seated l.,
holding sceptre, r. foot on prow, together
holding wreath inscribed VOT / XXXX; mint-
mark, *TES*. N, 4.60 gm. ↓.

1396 Miliarensis Constantinople, AD 351–5

Obv. D N CONSTANTIVS P F AVG. Bust, pearl-
diademed, draped, cuirassed, r.

Rev. VIRTVS EXERCITVS. Virtus standing facing,
head r., holding spear in r. hand, and resting
l. on shield; mint-mark, C·∈. Æ, 4.41 gm. ↑.

1397 Æ 4 Constantinople, AD 358–61

Obv. As No. 1396.

Rev. SPES REIPVBLICE. Emperor, helmeted and in
military dress, standing facing, head l.,
holding globe in r. hand, and spear in l.;
mint-mark, CONS∆ ✶. 2.33 gm. ↓.

1398 Solidus Nicomedia, AD 351

Obv. D N FL CL CONSTANTIVS NOB CAES. Bust of
Gallus, bare-headed, draped, cuirassed, r.

Rev. GLORIA REIPVBLICAE. Roma seated facing,
and Constantinopolis seated l., holding
sceptre in l. hand, r. foot on prow, together
holding wreath enclosing VO / TIS / V; mint-
mark, SMNB. N, 4.44 gm. ↓.

1399 Medallion Nicomedia, AD 355–61

Obv. D N CONSTANTIVS MAX AVG. Half-length
bust, three-quarters facing, helmeted, pearl-
diademed, and in cuirass ornamented with
Medusa head, holding Victory on globe in r.
hand, and spear over shoulder in l.

Rev. GLORIA ROMANORVM. Emperor, laureate and
draped, seated l., holding Victory on globe
and sceptre, r. foot on prow; mint-mark,
SMN. N, 20.22 gm. ↑.

A $4\frac{1}{2}$ solidus multiple.

1400 Aureus Antioch, AD 347–55

Obv. FL IVL CONSTANTIVS PERP AVG. Bust, pearl-diademed, draped, cuirassed, l.
Rev. GLORIA ROMANORVM. Emperor standing facing, head l., in facing quadriga, distributing largesse with his r. hand, and holding eagle-tipped sceptre in l.; mint-mark, SMANT. *N*, 5.36 gm. ↓.
NB The old *aureus* standard.

1401 Solidus Antioch, AD 343–50

Obv. As No. 1400, but bust r.
Rev. GLORIA REIPVBLICAE. Emperor riding r., greeted by turreted female figure l., holding r. hand, and torch in l.; mint-mark, SMANI; *N*, 4.40 gm. ↓.

1402 Nine siliquae Antioch, AD 351

Obv. CONSTANTIVS CAES. Bust of Gallus, bare-headed, draped, cuirassed, r.
Rev. VICTORIA AVGVSTORVM. Victory seated r. on cuirass, holding shield enclosing VO / TIS / V, and supported by Genius; mint-mark, SMAN. *N*, 1.64 gm. ↓.

1403 Medallion Antioch, AD 355–61

Obv. FL IVL CONSTANTIVS PERP AVG. Bust, in laureate and rosetted diadem, draped, cuirassed, l.
Rev. GLORIA ROMANORVM. Roma seated facing, holding Victory on globe and spear, and Constantinopolis seated l., r. foot on prow, holding Victory on globe and sceptre; mint-mark, ·SMANT·. *N*, 8.90 gm. ↓.
A double solidus multiple.

1404 Solidus Antioch, AD 355–61

Obv. FL IVL CONSTANTIVS PERP AVG. Bust, three-quarters facing, helmeted, pearl-diademed, cuirassed, with shield on l. shoulder, and holding spear over shoulder in r. hand.
Rev. GLORIA REIPVBLICAE. Roma seated facing, head r. and Constantinopolis seated l., holding sceptre in l. hand, r. foot on prow, together holding wreath enclosing VOT / XXX / MVLT / XXXX; mint-mark, SMANΔ·. *N*, 4.50 gm. ↓.
This obverse bust type introduced by Constantius II eventually became the standard portrait type on the gold coinage of the late empire and the early Byzantine empire.

7 Julian and Jovian, AD 360–364

After his proclamation in AD 360 Julian endeavoured to secure his recognition as an Augustus from Constantius II; when this was not forthcoming Julian began to march eastwards, but civil war was averted by the death of Constantius in AD 361. Julian's reign was marked by his efforts to restore the ancient pagan worship, but the attempt did not outlive the emperor. In AD 363 Julian embarked on a campaign against the Persians, but after initial success the Romans were halted at the battle of Maranga where Julian was wounded and died. Under Jovian, the captain of a senior regiment, proclaimed emperor in Julian's place, a dishonourable peace was arranged with the Persians, and the Roman army retreated. On the march back to Constantinople Jovian died in February, AD 364.

The same mints as in the previous period continued to operate under Julian, and in the Gallic mints under his control Julian initially coined for Constantius. The principal innovation was Julian's introduction of a large base metal coin of Æ 1 denomination which was also issued in Jovian's short reign.

Julian, AD 360–363

1405 Solidus Trier, AD 360

Obv. FL CL IVLIANVS PER AVG. Bust, pearl-diademed, draped, cuirassed, r.
Rev. GLORIA REIPVBLICAE. Roma seated facing, head l., and Constantinopolis, seated l., holding sceptre in l. hand, r. foot on prow, together holding wreath enclosing VOTIS / V / MVLTIS / X; mint-mark, TR·. N, 4.36 gm. ↓.

1406 Miliarensis Lyons, AD 360

Obv. D N CONSTANTIVS P F AVG. Bust, pearl-diademed, draped, cuirassed, r.
Rev. VIRTVS EXERCITVS. Virtus standing l., head r., holding spear in r. hand, and resting l. hand on shield; mint-mark, LVG. Æ, 4.6 gm. ↑.
Julian, after his proclamation as Augustus, for a time continued to coin in the name of Constantius.

1407 Solidus Arles, AD 362–3

Obv. FL CL IVLIANVS PFP AVG. Bust, pearl-diademed, bearded, draped, cuirassed, r.
Rev. VIRTVS EXERC GALL. Soldier standing r., head l., holding trophy over shoulder and placing r. hand on head of kneeling captive; to r., eagle to r., head l., with wreath in beak; mint-mark, KONSTÂN. N, 4.36 gm. ↓.
The reverse honours the army in Gaul which had proclaimed Julian Augustus.

1408 Siliqua Arles, AD 362–3

Obv. D N FL CL IVLIANVS P F AVG. As No. 1407.
Rev. Wreath with medallion enclosing eagle at top., enclosing VOT / X / MVLT / XX; mint-mark SCONST. Æ, 1.98 gm. ↑.

1409 Solidus Thessalonica, AD 361

Obv. FL CL IVLIANVS PP AVG. As No. 1407.
Rev. VIRTVS EXERCITVS ROMANI. As No. 1407, but
no eagle; mint-mark, TES Ω. *N*, 4.36 gm. ↓.
Coinage was struck for Julian by the mints which
came under his control on his march towards
Constantinople.

1410 Miliarensis Sirmium, AD 361

Obv. As No. 1409 but -PF AVG.
Rev. VICTORIA ROMANORVM. Under an arch
emperor standing l., head r., crowned by
Victory standing l., holding palm-branch in
l. hand; mint-mark, *SIRM. *R*, 4.52 gm. ↑.

1411 Æ 1 Constantinople, AD 362–3

Obv. As No. 1408.
Rev. SECVRITAS REIPVB. Bull, head facing, standing
r., above, two stars; mint-mark, ·CONSPΓ✷·.
8.73 gm. ↑.
This new large denomination, similar to that of
Magnentius (cf. No. 1365) was reintroduced by
Julian. The reverse type, the bull, is connected with
Julian's revival of pagan cults, but the identification
with Apis is doubtful.

1412 Solidus Antioch, AD 362–3

Obv. FL CL IVLIANVS P F AVG. Bust, pearl-
diademed, long beard, draped, cuirassed, r.
Rev. As No. 1409 but ROMANORVM; mint-mark,
ANTZ. *N*, 4.44 gm. ↓.

1413 Solidus Antioch, AD 363

Obv. FL CL IVLIANVS P F AVG. Bust, pearl-
diademed, long beard, mantled l., raising r.
hand and holding sceptre in l.
Rev. VIRTVS EXERCITVS ROMANORVM. Emperor, in
consular robes, seated facing, holding mappa
in r. hand and eagle-tipped sceptre in l.;
mint-mark, ANTA. *N*, 4.47 gm. ↓.
This solidus issued to mark Julian's fourth
consulship is unusual in showing the emperor as
consul on both obverse and reverse.

Jovian, AD 363–364

1414 Solidus Thessalonica, AD 363–4

Obv. D N IOVIANVS P F AVG. Bust, pearl-diademed,
draped, cuirassed, r.
Rev. SECVRITAS REIPVBLICE. Emperor standing l.,
holding standard with Chi-Rho in r. hand,
and globe in l.; to l., seated captive; mint-
mark, ·TES·. *N*, 4.58 gm. ↓.

1415 Solidus Constantinople, AD 363–4

Obv. D N IOVIANVS P F PERP AVG. As No. 1414, but
with laureate and rosetted diadem.

Rev. SECVRITAS REIPVBLICAE. Roma seated facing,
and Constantinopolis seated l., holding
sceptre in l. hand, r. foot on prow, together
holding wreath enclosing VOT / V / MVL / X;
mint-mark, CONSP. *N*, 4.42 gm. ↑.

1416 Æ 1 Constantinople, AD 363–4

Obv. D N IOVIANVS P F AVG. As No. 1415.

Rev. VICTORIA ROMANORVM. Emperor standing l.,
head r., holding standard, and Victory on
globe; mint-mark, CONSPB. 8.23 gm. ↓.

8 Valentinian I, Valens, and Gratian, AD 364–378

On the death of Jovian Valentinian I was proclaimed emperor, and very soon he appointed his brother Valens as his co-Augustus. Control of affairs in the East was entrusted to Valens, while Valentinian himself set off for Gaul to deal with barbarian unrest on the frontier. In AD 365 Procopius, a relative of the late emperor Julian, had himself proclaimed emperor in Constantinople, but after an initial success was defeated and put to death in AD 366. To ensure the succession Valentinian appointed his young son, Gratian, a co-Augustus in AD 367. Valentinian I's death in AD 375 was followed by the appointment of his infant son, Valentinian II, also as an Augustus. In AD 378 Valens, opposing the Gothic incursions into the Balkans, was defeated and killed at the battle of Adrianople.

The net-work of mints active in the previous period continued unchanged. In the monetary system the precious-metal denominations continued unchanged, and of the base-metal denominations the large Æ 1 piece of the coinage of Julian and Jovian was issued at the outset of the joint reign of Valentinian I and Valens, but the common denomination throughout the reign was the small Æ 3 piece.

1417 Solidus Trier, AD 364–7

Obv. D N VALENTINIANVS P F AVG. Bust, pearl-diademed, draped, cuirassed, r.
Rev. RESTITVTOR REIPVBLICAE. Emperor standing facing, head r., holding standard with Chi-Rho in r. hand, and Victory on globe in l.; mint-mark, TR. N, 4.36 gm. ↓.

1418 Solidus Trier, AD 367

Obv. D N GRATIANVS P F AVG. Bust, pearl-diademed, draped, cuirassed, r.
Rev. PRINCIPIVM IVVENTVTIS. Emperor, nimbate, standing r., holding spear in r. hand, and globe in l.; mint-mark, SMTR. N, 4.47 gm. ↓.

The reverse inscription presents a different form of the more usual *Princeps Iuventutis*, the traditional title of the heir-apparent.

1419 Solidus Trier, AD 367–75

Obv. D N VALENS P F AVG. Bust, helmeted, pearl-diademed, draped, cuirassed, l., with spear and decorated shield.
Rev. VICTORES AVGVSTI. Valentinian I and Gratian seated facing, together holding globe; above, Victory flying l., crowns them; mint-mark, TR·OB. N, 4.40 gm. ↓.

The identification of the two figures on the reverse as Valentinian I and Gratian is suggested by the fact that the figure on the right is much smaller than the other.

1420 Solidus Trier, AD 362–75

Obv. D N VALENS P F AVG. Bust, pearl-diademed, draped, cuirassed, r.
Rev. VICTORIA AVGG. As No. 1419, but Victory is shown as a facing half-figure with outspread wings; between the seated figures, a palm-branch; mint-mark, TROBS. N, 4.48 gm. ↓.

A final letter is added to the mint-mark of the group to mark the officina which struck the coin, in this case s for the second officina.

1421 Nine siliquae Trier, AD 367–75

Obv. As No. 1418, but laureate-rosetted diadem.
Rev. VICTORIA AVGVSTORVM. Victory advancing l., holding wreath and palm; mint-mark, TROB. *N*, 1.66 gm. ↑.

1422 Medallion Trier, AD 367–75

Obv. D N VALENS P F AVG. Bust, pearl-diademed, draped, cuirassed, r.
Rev. TRIVMFATOR GENT BARB. Emperor standing facing, head l., holding standard with Chi-Rho in r. hand, and globe in l.; to l., kneeling captive; mint-mark, TRPS·. *R*, 13.45 gm. ↑.
A silver multiple of 4 siliquae.

1423 Miliarensis Trier, AD 368–9

Obv. D N VALENTINIANVS P F AVG. Bust, pearl-diademed, draped, cuirassed, r.
Rev. Wreath enclosing VOTIS / V / MVLTIS / X; mint-mark, TRPS·. *R*, 5.1 gm. ↑.
A 'heavy' miliarensis, recording the vota for Valentinian's quinquennalia.

1424 Miliarensis Trier, AD 367–75

Obv. D N GRATIANVS P F AVG. Bust, pearl-diademed, draped, cuirassed, r.
Rev. VIRTVS EXERCITVS. Emperor standing facing, head l., holding standard with Chi-Rho in r. hand, and resting l. hand on shield; mint-mark, TRPS·. *R*, 4.30 gm. ↑.
A 'light' miliarensis.

1425 Siliqua Trier, AD 362–75

Obv. D N VALENS P F AVG. Bust, pearl-diademed, draped, cuirassed, r.
Rev. VRBS ROMA. Roma seated l., holding Victory on globe in r. hand, and spear in l.; mint-mark, TRPS·. *R*, 2.07 gm. ↑.

1426 Semissis Trier, AD 372–3

Obv. D N GRATIANVS P F AVG. Bust, rosette-diademed, draped, cuirassed, r.
Rev. VICTORIA AVGVSTORVM. Victory seated r. on cuirass holding wreath enclosing VOT / V / MVLT / X supported by Genius; mint-mark, TROBT. *N*, 2.23 gm. ↑.

1427 Solidus Trier, AD 373–4

Obv. As No. 1417.
Rev. GLORIA REIPVBLICAE. Roma seated facing,
and Constantinopolis seated l., holding
sceptre in l. hand, r. foot on prow, together
holding wreath enclosing VOT / X / MVLT /
XV; mint-mark, TROB. *N*, 4.43 gm. ↑.
About AD 368 the letters OB = obryzum, pure gold,
began to be added to the mint signature, first at
Constantinople and subsequently at other mints.

1428 Solidus Trier, AD 375–8

Obv. D N VALENTINIANVS IVN P F AVG. Bust, pearl-
diademed, draped, cuirassed, r.
Rev. VICTORIA AVGG. Two emperors seated
facing, together holding globe; above, half-
length figure of Victory facing, with
outspread wings; between two figures,
palm-branch; mint-mark, TROBC.
N, 4.42 gm. ↓.
The letter C in the mint-mark here indicates the first
officina.

1429 Nine siliquae Lyons, AD 364–7

Obv. D N VALENTINIANVS P F AVG. Bust, pearl-
diademed, draped, cuirassed, r.
Rev. VICTORIA DD NN AVG. Victory advancing l.,
with wreath and palm-branch; in field l.,
star; mint-mark, $\frac{*\,|}{\text{LVG}}$.

N, 2.06 gm. ↓.

1430 Miliarensis Lyons, AD 366

Obv. D N VALENTINIANVS P F AVG. Bust, pearl-
diademed, draped, cuirassed, r.
Rev. SALVS REIPVBLICAE. Four standards; mint-
mark, LVG. Æ, 5.69 gm. ↓.
The reverse type of this 'heavy' miliarensis may
commemorate Roman military success against
barbarian invaders of Gaul.

1431 Miliarensis Arles, AD 364–7

Obv. D N VALENS P F AVG. Bust, pearl-diademed,
draped, cuirassed, r.
Rev. RESTITVTOR REIP. Emperor standing facing,
head r., holding standard with Chi-Rho in
r. hand, and Victory on globe in l.; mint-
mark, PCONST. Æ, 4.58 gm. ↑.
This 'light' miliarensis uses at Arles the reverse type
common on early solidi of the joint reign of
Valentinian and Valens.

1432 Siliqua Arles, AD 364–7

Obv. D N VALENTINIANVS P F AVG. Bust, pearl-
diademed, draped, cuirassed, r.
Rev. As No. 1431, but mint-mark $\frac{\text{OF}|\text{III}}{\text{CONST}}$.

Æ. 2.09 gm. ↓.
In this coinage the mark of the officina is given in a
more explicit form than usual.

1433 Solidus Arles, AD 367–75

Obv. DN GRATIANVS AVGG AVG. Bust, pearl-diademed, draped, cuirassed, r.

Rev. GLORIA NOVI SAECVLI. Emperor standing facing, head l., holding Victory on globe in r. hand, and standard with Chi-Rho surmounted by Victory. Both Victories crown the emperor; mint-mark, KONSTAN.
N, 4.46 gm. ↓.

On some early coinage of Gratian at this mint as well as at Lyons he is given the unusual title *Augg Aug*, presumably *Augustorum Augustus*. The reverse type stresses the hopes for the future represented by the youthful emperor.

1434 Æ 3 Arles, AD 367–75

Obv. As No. 1433.

Rev. GLORIA NOVI SAECVLI. Emperor standing facing, head l., holding standard with Chi-Rho in r. hand, and resting l. on shield; mint-mark, $\frac{N|}{TCON}$.

2.86 gm. ↓.

In the Æ 3 coinage at Arles Gratian has his own special reverse (cf. No. 1433)

1435 Æ 3 Arles, AD 368–75

Obv. DN VALENS P F AVG. Bust, pearl-diademed, draped, cuirassed, r.

Rev. SECVRITAS REIPVBLICAE. Victory advancing l. with wreath and palm; mint-mark, SCON.
2.42 gm. ↓.

This is an example of one of two very common reverses on the Æ 3 coinage of this period (see also No. 1440).

1436 Medallion Milan, AD 364

Obv. D N VALENTINIANVS P F AVG. Bust, pearl-diademed, draped, cuirassed, r.

Rev. FELIX ADVENTVS AVG M. Emperor riding l., raising r. hand; mint-mark, MED.
N, 6.68 gm. ↓.

A multiple of $1\frac{1}{2}$ solidi struck to commemorate Valentinian's arrival in Milan in October, AD 364.

1437 Nine-siliquae Rome, AD 364–7

Obv. D N VALENS P F AVG. Bust, pearl-diademed, draped, cuirassed, r.

Rev. VICTORIA AVGVSTI N. Victory advancing l., with wreath and palm; mint-mark, ↘R·.
N, 1.65 gm. ↓.

1438 Miliarensis Rome, AD 364

Obv. As No. 1437 but undraped.

Rev. VICTORIA AVGVSTORVM. Victory standing r., l. foot on globe, inscribing VOT / V / MVLT / X on shield set on column; mint-mark, RQ.
Æ, 4.58 gm. ↑.

The *vota* here must be the *vota suscepta* at the inception of the reign.

1439 Miliarensis Siscia, AD 364–7

Obv. As No. 1437.

Rev. GLORIA ROMANORVM. Two emperors standing facing, heads turned towards each other, each holding standard with Chi-Rho and globe; mint-mark, ·SIS∗. Æ, 4.38 gm. ↓.

1440 Æ 3 Siscia, AD 364–7

Obv. As No. 1437.

Rev. GLORIA ROMANORVM. Emperor advancing r., with r. hand dragging captive, and holding standard with Chi-Rho in l., mint-mark, ↘ BSISC. 2.29 gm. ↓.

This is one of the two very common reverses on the Æ 3 coinage of this period (see also No. 1435).

1441 Æ I Sirmium, AD 364–7

Obv. D N VALENTINIANVS P F AVG. Bust, pearl-diademed, draped, cuirassed, r.

Rev. RESTITVTOR REIPVBLICAE. Emperor standing facing, head r., holding standard in r. hand, and Victory on globe in l.; mint-mark, ASIRM. 8.62 gm. ↑.

An example of the last Æ I denomination issued by Valentinian I and Valens in the early coinage of the reign.

1442 Solidus Thessalonica, AD 365

Obv. D N VALENS P F AVG. Bust, pearl-diademed, draped, mantled, l., holding mappa in r. hand and sceptre in l.

Rev. SPES REIP. Emperor standing facing, head r., holding standard with Chi-Rho in r. hand, and Victory on globe in l., and spurning kneeling captive; mint-mark,

| ‡ .
SMTES

N, 4.48 gm. ↑.

The occasion of this issue was the first consulship of Valens in AD 365.

1443 Æ 3 Heraclea, AD 365–6

Obv. D N PROCOPIVS P F AVG. Bust, pearl-diademed, draped, cuirassed, l.

Rev. REPARATIO FEL TEMP. Emperor standing facing, head r., holding standard with Chi-Rho in r. hand, and resting l. hand on shield; in field high r., Chi-Rho; mint-mark, SMHΓ, 3.12 gm. ↑.

An example of the Æ 3 denomination with its special type for Procopius struck while the mint of Heraclea was under his control.

1444 Aureus Constantinople, AD 365

Obv. D N VALENTINIANVS P F AVG. Bust, pearl-diademed, draped, cuirassed, l.

Rev. GLORIA ROMANORVM. Emperor, nimbate, in facing quadriga, with r. hand scattering coins, and in l. holding on globe Victory who crowns him; mint-mark, CONSP. N, 5.35 gm. ↓.

Although the obverse does not show the emperor in consular dress, the reverse shows Valentinian distributing largesse in the consular procession.

1445 Solidus Constantinople, AD 364–7

Obv. D N VALENS P F AVG. Bust, pearl-diademed, draped, cuirassed, r.
Rev. VIRTVS ROMANORVM. Two emperors standing facing, heads turned towards each other, each holding spear, and together holding on globe Victory who crowns them; mint-mark, ⤾ CONS ⤢ . *N*, 4.50 gm. ↑.

1446 Miliarensis Constantinople, AD 364–7

Obv. D N VALENTINIANVS P F AVG. Bust, pearl-diademed, draped, cuirassed, r.
Rev. SECVRITAS REIP. Two emperors standing facing, heads turned towards each other, each holding standard with Chi-Rho, and together holding on globe Victory who crowns them; mint-mark, CONSPB. *R*, 5.12 gm. ↑.

1447 Solidus Constantinople, AD 365–6

Obv. D N PROCOPIVS P F AVG. Bust, pearl-diademed, draped, cuirassed, r.
Rev. SECVRITAS REIPVB. Emperor standing l., head r., holding spear in r. hand, and resting l. on shield; mint-mark, CONS. *N*, 4.46 gm. ↓.
Procopius revolted in AD 365 in Constantinople when Valentinian I was in Gaul and Valens in Asia.

1448 Solidus Constantinople, AD 368

Obv. D N VALENS P F AVG. Bust, pearl-diademed, mantled, l., holding mappa in r. hand, and sceptre in l.
Rev. VOTA PVBLICA. Two emperors, nimbate, seated facing, each holding mappa and sceptre, to r. and l., seated captive; mint-mark, *CONS Ω . *N*, 4.42 gm. ↓.
As the form of mint-mark appears on coins of Gratian the issue must be after AD 367, and this solidus was probably struck for the second consulship of Valens in AD 368.

1449 Solidus Constantinople, AD 368–9

Obv. D N GRATIANVS P F AVG. Bust, rosette-diademed, draped, cuirassed, r.
Rev. VICTORIA AVGVSTORVM. Victory seated r. on cuirass, shield behind, inscribing VOT / V / MVLT / X on shield set on column; mint-mark, $\frac{\text{O} \mid \text{B}}{\text{CONS*}}$.
N, 4.46 gm. ↑.
The *vota* here recorded are those for the quinquennalia of the senior emperors in AD 368–9. This is probably the first appearance of the formula OB = *obryzum*, pure gold, on gold coins.

1450 Nine siliquae Nicomedia, AD 364–7

Obv. D N VALENS P F AVG. Bust, pearl-diademed, draped, cuirassed, r.
Rev. RESTITVTOR REIP. Emperor standing facing, head l., holding standard with Chi-Rho; mint-mark, SMN. *N*, 1.67 gm. ↑.
The reverse type on this denomination is a simpler version of the type on the solidus.

1451 Solidus Nicomedia, AD 368

Obv. D N VALENS P F AVG. Bust, pearl-diademed, mantled, l., holding mappa and sceptre.

Rev. VOTA PVBLICA. Two emperors nimbate, seated facing, each holding mappa and sceptre; in ex., between letters of mint-mark, seated captives; mint-mark, S–MN–M. *N*, 4.32 gm. ↓.

The occasion for this issue was probably the second consulship of Valens, held jointly with Valentinian I in AD 368.

1452 Solidus Antioch, AD 364–7

Obv. D N VALENS PER F AVG. Bust, pearl-diademed, draped, cuirassed, r.

Rev. RESTITVTOR REIPVBLICAE. Emperor standing facing, head r., holding standard with cross in r. hand, and Victory on globe in l.; mint-mark, ·ANTI. *N*, 4.48 gm. ↓.

This reverse type on the earliest gold coinage of the reign was issued with great frequency at Antioch.

1453 Solidus Antioch, AD 368–9

Obv. D N VALENTINIANVS P F AVG. Bust, rosette-diademed, draped and cuirassed, r.

Rev. SPES R P. Two emperors, nimbate, seated facing, each holding globe and long sceptre; between them, a small standing figure with, above, a shield inscribed VOT / V / MVL / X; mint-mark, ANTA+. *N*, 4.04 gm. ↓.

The small figure in the centre on this dynastic reverse is the young Gratian, appointed Augustus in AD 367.

1454 Solidus Antioch, AD 373–4

Obv. D N VALENS PER F AVG. Bust, pearl-diademed, draped, cuirassed, r.

Rev. VICTORIA AVGVSTORVM. Victory seated r. on cuirass, shield behind, inscribing VOT / X / MVL / XX on shield held on knee; in field r., Chi-Rho; mint-mark, ANOBΔ. *N*, 4.36 gm. ↑.

The appearance of the formula OB on gold coins of Antioch is connected with types celebrating the senior emperor's decennalia in AD 373–4.

1455 Medallion Antioch, AD 373–4

Obv. D N VALENS PER F AVG. Bust, rosette-diademed, draped, cuirassed, r.

Rev. GLORIA ROMANORVM. Emperor riding l., raising r. hand; mint-mark, $\frac{+|}{ANOBS}$.

N, 6.72 gm. ↑.
A multiple of 1½ solidi.

9 Gratian, Valentinian II, and Theodosius I, AD 378–395

In AD 379 Gratian, as Senior Augustus, appointed Theodosius as an Augustus to take charge of the eastern provinces, while he himself continued to control the western provinces, with the young Valentinian II in nominal charge of Italy and Illyricum. In AD 383 Magnus Maximus, commander in Britain, having revolted, declared himself Augustus and crossed to Gaul where Gratian was captured and put to death. Maximus invaded Italy in AD 387, and Valentinian II fled to Thessalonica to the protection of Theodosius. It was not until the next year that Theodosius marched against Maximus, but by mid-AD 388 Maximus surrendered at Aquileia and was put to death. Theodosius in the meantime had raised his elder son, Arcadius, to the rank of Augustus in AD 383. In AD 391 Theodosius returned to Constantinople, and in the next year the Frankish general, Arbogast, procured the death of Valentinian II and the appointment of the usurper, Eugenius, as the Augustus of the West. Theodosius, having also appointed his younger son, Honorius, an Augustus in AD 393, marched again into Italy where at the battle of the Frigidus in AD 394 Eugenius was defeated and slain. Theodosius was left as the last effective sole ruler of the empire, but only for a brief period until his death in early AD 395.

In the mint system the only notable innovation was the brief re-opening of the London mint by Magnus Maximus, possibly to produce the first coinage in his name on his proclamation in Britain. In the monetary system a new small gold denomination, the tremissis or third of a solidus (of an average weight of 1.51 gm.), was introduced by Theodosius I, in place of the 9 siliquae piece (or $1\frac{1}{2}$ scripulum), and was to become in the later empire an increasingly important denomination. In silver the very rare half-siliqua made its appearance in this period. In the base-metal coinage the Æ 1 denomination was struck so rarely that it is probably to be classed as medallic, rather than an integral part of the coinage system. At the outset of the period the common bronze was the Æ 3, but the Æ 2 was revived by Gratian, and, though it disappeared in the West under Magnus Maximus, it continued in the East down to the death of Theodosius. In AD 379 Gratian added a smaller Æ 4 piece, of an average weight of 1.49 gm., initially with *vota* reverses,

but towards the end of the period commonly with a Victory type.

1456 **Solidus** London, AD 383

Obv. D N MAG MAXIMVS P F AVG. Bust, with laureate-rosetted diadem, draped, cuirassed, r.
Rev. VICTORIA AVGG. Two emperors seated facing enthroned, together holding globe; behind, half-length figure of Victory facing with outstretched wings; below, between emperors, palm-branch; mint-mark, AVGOB. *N*, 4.44 gm. ↓.

The mint signature AVG is an abbreviation for Augusta, the name by which London had come to be known at this time. The rarity of coinage in gold and silver (see below) from London suggests that the mint's activity was short-lived.

1457 **Siliqua** London, AD 383

Obv. As No. 1456 but pearl-diademed.
Rev. VICTORIA AVGG. Victory advancing l., holding wreath and palm-branch; mint-mark, AVGPS. Æ, 1.76 gm. ↑.
See No. 1456.

1458 Solidus Trier, AD 378–83

Obv. D N GRATIANVS P F AVG. Bust, pearl-diademed, mantled l., holding mappa in r. hand, and sceptre in l.

Rev. VOTA PVBLICA. Gratian and Valentinian II, nimbate, seated facing enthroned, Gratian holding mappa aloft in r. hand and globe in l., Valentinian II holding mappa against breast in r. hand, and globe in l.; mint-mark, TROBT. *N*, 4.48 gm. ↓.

The precise occasion of the issue of this consular solidus is unclear. Since the reverse shows the emperor Valentinian II, the occasion cannot be Gratian's joint consulship with Theodosius in AD 380.

1459 Siliqua Trier, AD 379–83

Obv. D N THEODOSIVS P F AVG. Bust, pearl-diademed, draped, cuirassed, r.

Rev. PERPETVETAS. Phoenix standing l. on globe; mint-mark, TRPS. *R*, 1.78 gm. ↑.

The phoenix, symbolic of renewal and continuity, was chosen as an apt type for the newly appointed emperor, Theodosius.

1460 Solidus Trier, AD 383

Obv. D N MAG MAXIMVS P F AVG. Bust, rosette-diademed, draped, cuirassed, r.

Rev. RESTITVTOR REIPVBLICAE. Emperor standing facing, head r., holding standard in r. hand, and Victory on globe in l.; mint-mark, $\overset{*|}{\text{SMTR}}$. *N*, 4.42 gm. ↑.

For his earliest gold coinage at Trier Maximus revived the earlier reverse type of Valentinian I.

1461 Tremissis Trier, AD 383–8

Obv. D N MAG MAXIMVS P F AVG. Bust, pearl-diademed, draped, cuirassed, r.

Rev. VICTORIA AVGVSTORVM. Victory advancing l., holding wreath in r. hand, and palm-branch in l.; mint-mark, SMTR. *N*, 1.51 gm. ↓.

The recently introduced denomination, the tremissis, continued the reverse type used on the 9 siliqua piece or $1\frac{1}{2}$ scripulum which it displaced.

1462 Solidus Trier, AD 386–92

Obv. D N THEODOSIVS P F AVG. Bust, pearl-diademed, draped, cuirassed, r.

Rev. VICTORIA AVGG. Two emperors, nimbate, seated facing enthroned, together holding globe; behind, half-length figure of Victory with outstretched wings; below, between emperors, palm-branch; mint-mark, $\dfrac{\text{T}|\text{R}}{\text{COM}}$. *N*, 4.45 gm. ↑.

1463 Medallion Trier, AD 392–4

Obv. D N EVGENIVS P F AVG. Bust, pearl-diademed, draped, cuirassed, r.

Rev. GLORIA ROMANORVM. Roma seated facing, holding Victory on globe and sceptre, and Constantinopolis seated l., holding Victory on globe and cornucopiae, r. foot on prow; mint-mark, $\dfrac{\text{T}|\text{R}}{\text{COM}}$. *N*, 8.90 gm. ↑.

A double solidus of Eugenius, usurper in the West.

1464 Miliarensis Trier, AD 392–4

Obv. As No. 1463.
Rev. VIRTVS EXERCITVS. Emperor standing l., holding standard in r. hand, and resting l. on shield; mint-mark, TRPS. Æ, 4.42 gm. ↓.

1465 Siliqua Lyons, AD 378–83

Obv. D N VALENTINIANVS IVN P F AVG. Bust, pearl-diademed, draped, cuirassed, r.
Rev. VICTORIA AVGGG. Victory advancing l., holding wreath in r. hand, and palm-branch in l.; mint-mark, LVGPS. Æ, 1.96 gm. ↓.
Though Valentinian I was now dead, Valentinian II's titulature still included the distinctive *Iunior*. In the reverse inscription the abbreviation *Auggg* for Augustorum has three Gs to indicate the college of three emperors.

1466 Solidus Lyons, AD 388–92

Obv. DN VALENTINIANVS P F AVG. Bust, pearl-diademed, draped, cuirassed, r.
Rev. VICTORIA AVGG. Two emperors, nimbate, seated facing enthroned, together holding globe; behind, half-length figure of Victory with outspread wings; below, between emperors, palm-branch; mint-mark, L|D .
                                 COM
  Ν, 4.48 gm. ↑.
After the defeat of Magnus Maximus, Valentinian II was resident in Gaul.

1467 Miliarensis Lyons, AD 388–92

Obv. As No. 1466.
Rev. GLORIA ROMANORVM. Emperor standing facing, head l., holding standard with r. hand, and resting l. on shield; mint-mark, LVGPS. Æ, 4.16 gm. ↓.

1468 Æ 4 Lyons, AD 388–92

Obv. As No. 1466.
Rev. VICTORIA AVGGG. Victory advancing l., holding wreath in r. hand, and palm-branch in l.; mint-mark, LVGP. 1.23 gm. ↓.
The smallest bronze denomination, the Æ 4, commonly has a Victory reverse type in this period.

1469 Siliqua Lyons, AD 392–4

Obv. D N EVGENIVS P F AVG. Bust, pearl-diademed, draped, cuirassed, r.
Rev. VRBS ROMA. Roma seated l. on cuirass, holding Victory on globe in r. hand, and spear in l.; mint-mark, LVGPS. Æ, 2.05 gm. ↑.
The Lyons mint also struck coinage for Eugenius, usurper in Gaul.

1470 Solidus Arles, AD 383–8

Obv. D N MAG MAXIMVS P F AVG. Bust, rosette-diademed, draped, cuirassed, r.
Rev. VICTORIA AVGG. As No. 1466, but no palm-branch between emperors, and mint mark, KONOB. N, 4.10 gm. ↓.

Although Maximus issued no coinage at Arles in the names of the legitimate emperors, the reverse here shows two emperors of equal stature, and suggests that Maximus still accorded recognition to them.

1471 Æ 4 Arles, AD 387–8

Obv. D N FL VICTOR P F AVG. Bust, pearl-diademed, draped, cuirassed, r.
Rev. SPES ROMANORVM. Camp-gate with two turrets; star between; mint-mark, PCON. 1.15 gm. ↑.

As coins of this type are also issued for Maximus' son, Flavius Victor, the issue must be dated to AD 387 when Victor was appointed Augustus.

1472 Miliarensis Rome, AD 378–83

Obv. D N VALENTINIANVS P F AVG. Bust, pearl-diademed, draped, cuirassed, r.
Rev. VICTORIA AVGVSTORVM. Victory advancing r., head l., dragging captive with r. hand, and holding trophy in l.; mint-mark, RP. Æ, 5.16 gm. ↓.

A 'heavy' miliarensis.

1473 Æ 1 Rome, AD 378–83

Obv. D N VALENTINIANVS P F AVG. Bust, helmeted, cuirassed, r., holding in r. hand sceptre surmounted by Chi-Rho, and in l., shield.
Rev. GLORIA ROMANORVM. Roma seated l. on shield, holding Victory on globe in r. hand, and spear in l.; mint-mark, SMRQ. Æ, 6.22 gm. ↓.

In view of the great rarity of such coins, they probably are to be regarded as medallic rather than as examples of an Æ 1 denomination.

1474 Solidus Milan, AD 387–8

Obv. D N FL VICTOR P F AVG. Bust, pearl-diademed, draped, cuirassed, r.
Rev. BONO REIPVBLICE NATI. Two emperors, the one on r. smaller, nimbate, seated facing enthroned, the smaller holding mappa in r. hand and together holding globe; behind, half-length figure of Victory with outspread wings; below, between emperors, palm-branch; mint-mark, MDOB. N, 4.48 gm. ↓.

The reverse inscription provides an unusual description of the emperors, Maximus and his son, Flavius Victor, appointed an Augustus in AD 387: 'Born for the good of the State.'

1475 Siliqua Milan, AD 387–8

Obv. D N MAG MAXIMVS P F AVG. Bust, pearl-diademed, draped, cuirassed, r.
Rev. VIRTVS ROMANORVM. Roma seated facing, head l., holding globe in r. hand, and spear in l.; mint-mark, MDPS. Æ, 1.47 gm. ↑.

1476 Solidus Milan, AD 390

Obv. D N VALENTINIANVS P F AVG. Bust, pearl-
diademed, mantled, l., holding mappa in r.
hand, and sceptre in l.

Rev. VOTA PVBLICA. Two emperors, nimbate,
seated facing, enthroned, each holding
mappa and sceptre; mint-mark, M|D .
COM

N, 4.52 gm. ↓.

This consular solidus commemorates Valentinian II's
fourth consulship in AD 390.

1477 Solidus Milan, AD 393–4

Obv. D N EVGENIVS P F AVG. Bust, pearl-diademed,
draped, cuirassed, r.

Rev. VICTORIA AVGG. Two emperors, nimbate,
seated facing, enthroned, together holding
globe; behind, half-length figure of
Victory with outspread wings; below,
between emperors, palm-branch; mint-
mark, M|D .
COM

N, 4.54 gm. ↑.

The mint of Milan came under the control of
Eugenius when he invaded north Italy in AD 393.

1478 Solidus Milan, AD 394–5

Obv. D N THEODOSIVS P F AVG. Bust, pearl-
diademed, draped, cuirassed, r.

Rev. VICTORIA AVGGG. Emperor standing r.
holding standard in r. hand, and Victory
on globe in l., and trampling on captive;
mint-mark, M|D .
COM

N, 4.39 gm. ↓.

Coinage was resumed at Milan for Theodosius and
his two sons after the defeat of Eugenius.

1479 Solidus Aquileia, AD 378–83

Obv. D N VALENTINIANVS IVN P F AVG. Bust, pearl-
diademed, draped, cuirassed, r.

Rev. VICTORIA AVGG. As No. 1477, but emperor
on r. also holds mappa in l. hand; mint-
mark, AQOBF. *N*, 4.44 gm. ↑.

The junior status of the young Valentinian II is
emphasised by the continued inclusion of *Iunior* in
his titulature, and the use of an unbroken obverse
inscription.

1480 Siliqua Aquileia, AD 378–83

Obv. D N GRATIANVS P F AVG. Bust, pearl-
diademed, draped, cuirassed, r.

Rev. VICTORIA AVGVSTORVM. Victory advancing l.,
holding wreath in r. hand, and palm-branch
in l.; mint-mark, AQPS. Æ, 3.35 gm. ↓.

The siliqua on the heavy standard of 96 to the pound
was superseded in about AD 355 by the lighter
siliqua, but makes isolated appearances at western
mints later on as in this instance.

1481 Æ 2 Siscia, AD 379–83

Obv. D N VALENTINIANVS IVN P F AVG. Bust, pearl-diademed, draped, cuirassed, r.
Rev. REPARATIO REIPVB. Emperor standing facing, head l., with r. hand raising kneeling turreted woman, and holding Victory on globe in l.; mint-mark, ASISC. 4.79 gm. ↓.

The Æ 2 denomination of bronze coinage was revived again by Gratian in AD 379.

1482 Solidus Sirmium, AD 393–5

Obv. D N HONORIVS P F AVG. Bust, pearl-diademed, draped, cuirassed, r.
Rev. VICTORIA AVGGG. Emperor standing r., holding standard in r. hand, and Victory on globe in l., and trampling on captive; mint-mark, $\frac{\text{S} \mid \text{M}}{\text{COMOB}}$.

N, 4.48 gm. ↑.

Honorius, appointed Augustus in AD 393, shared in this issue together with Theodosius and Arcadius.

1483 Solidus Thessalonica, AD 378–83

Obv. D N THEODOSIVS P F AVG. Bust, pearl-diademed, draped, cuirassed, r.
Rev. VICTORIA AVGG. Two emperors seated facing, enthroned, together holding globe; behind, half-length figure of Victory with outspread wings; below, between emperors, palm-branch; mint-mark, TESOB.
N, 4.48 gm. ↑.

1484 Æ 2 Thessalonica, AD 383–8

Obv. D N THEODOSIVS P F AVG. Bust, helmeted, and with pearl-diadem, draped, cuirassed, r., holding spear in r. hand, and shield in l.
Rev. GLORIA ROMANORVM. Emperor standing l., head r., on ship, raising r. hand; Victory seated at helm; mint-mark, $\frac{\Omega \mid}{\text{TESB}}$.

4.59 gm. ↓.

The Æ 2 denomination disappeared in the West under Magnus Maximus, but it continued to be issued by Balkan and eastern mints.

1485 Solidus Thessalonica, AD 388–93

Obv. D N ARCADIVS P F AVG. Bust, pearl-diademed, draped, cuirassed, r.
Rev. CONCORDIA AVGGG. Constantinopolis, seated facing, enthroned, head r., holding sceptre in r. hand, and globe in l., r. foot on prow; mint-mark, COMOB. *N*, 4.55 gm. ↑.

This issue is unusual in that a specific identification of the mint by inclusion of initial or other letters in the mint-mark is omitted. It is attributed on the grounds of style.

1486 Æ 2 Heraclea, AD 383–8

Obv. AEL FLACCILLA AVG. Bust with elaborate head-dress, draped, r.
Rev. SALVS REIPVBLICAE. Empress standing facing, head r., with arms crossed on breast; mint-mark, $\frac{* \mid +}{\cdot \text{SMHA}}$.

6.69 gm. ↑.

1487 Solidus Constantinople, AD 378–83

Obv. D N GRATIANVS P F AVG. Bust, rosette-
diademed, draped, cuirassed, r.

Rev. CONCORDIA AVGGG H. Constantinopolis
seated facing, enthroned, head r., holding
sceptre in r. hand, and globe in l., r. foot on
prow; mint-mark, CONOB. N, 4.48 gm. ↑.

The officinae producing this gold coinage at
Constantinople are marked by the addition to the
reverse inscription of the officina number in Greek
numerals.

1488 Solidus Constantinople, AD 379–83

Obv. AEL FLACCILLA AVG. Bust with elaborate
head-dress, draped, r.

Rev. SALVS REIPVBLICAE S. Victory seated r.,
inscribing Chi-Rho on shield held on knee;
mint-mark, CONOB. N, 4.47 gm. ↑.

The officina producing this coinage for Flaccilla is
also noted at the end of the reverse inscription.

1489 Æ 3 Constantinople, AD 379–83

Obv. D N THEODOSIVS P F AVG. Bust, rosette-
diademed, draped, cuirassed, r.

Rev. CONCORDIA AVGGG. As No. 1487;
mint-mark, $\frac{\text{⸽ | I}}{\text{CONSB}}$.

2.53 gm. ↓.

The Concordia type used on gold was commonly
used on the Æ 3 denominations at eastern mints.

1490 Tremissis Constantinople, AD 383–8

Obv. D N VALENTINIANVS P F AVG. Bust, pearl-
diademed, draped, cuirassed, r.

Rev. VICTORIA AVGVSTORVM. Victory advancing
l., holding wreath in r. hand, and cross on
globe in l.; mint-mark, CONOB.
N, 1.50 gm. ↓.

The tremissis, or third of a solidus, introduced in
this period, ousted the earlier small gold coin, the $1\frac{1}{2}$
scripulum.

1491 Solidus Antioch, AD 379

Obv. D N VALENTINIANVS IVN P F AVG. Bust, pearl-
diademed, draped, cuirassed, r.

Rev. Victory seated r. on cuirass, inscribing
VOT / V on shield held on knee; mint-mark,
$\frac{\text{| ✳}}{\text{ANOBI}}$.

N, 4.49 gm. ↓.

This coinage commemorated the celebration of
Valentinian II's quinquennial vows in this year.

1492 Æ 2 Antioch, AD 383

Obv. D N ARCADIVS P F AVG. Bust, rosette-
diademed, draped, cuirassed, r., holding
spear in r. hand, and shield in l.; above, hand
holding wreath.

Rev. GLORIA ROMANORVM. Emperor standing
facing, head l., holding standard in r. hand,
and resting l. on shield; to l., kneeling
captive; mint-mark, ✳ANTS. 6.22 gm. ↓.

A novel feature on the obverse of this Æ 2
denomination is the hand with wreath, presumably
the hand of God.

1493 Æ 4 Antioch, AD 383–92

Obv. D N THEODOSIVS P F AVG. Bust, pearl-diademed, draped, cuirassed, r.

Rev. SALVS REIPVBLICAE. Victory advancing l., holding trophy on shoulder with r. hand, and dragging captive with l.; mint-mark, $\underset{\text{ANTB}}{+|}$.

1.66 gm. ↑.

This reverse is one of the most common types used on the Æ 4 denomination towards the end of this period.

1494 Æ 2 Alexandria, AD 385–8

Obv. D N ARCADIVS P F AVG. Bust, pearl-diademed, draped, cuirassed, r.

Rev. VIRTS EXERCITI. Emperor standing r., holding standard in r. hand, and globe in l.; l. foot on captive; mint-mark, ALEΓ. 4.97 gm. ↓.

This new reverse for the Æ 2 denomination in some eastern mints was introduced in AD 385. Note the error in the reverse inscription – VIRTS for VIRTUS.

10 The Divided Empire, AD 395–498

From the death of Theodosius I in AD 395 the empire was in effect divided into two, an eastern empire with its capital in Constantinople, and a western empire with its capital in Italy, initially at Milan, but later at Ravenna where the imperial court settled. In practice the emperor in the East was regarded as the senior, and indeed the eastern empire in this period succeeded in maintaining its territory against barbarian onslaught. In the West the empire was gradually eroded by barbarian conquest of the provinces until little but Italy remained. Italy also was finally overrun, and a sequence of ephemeral and ineffective western emperors finally came to an end in AD 476 when Odovacar, king of the Heruli, deposed Romulus Augustulus and was recognised as overlord of Italy by the eastern emperor, Zeno, who conferred on him the title of Patrician. It seems that Odovacar may have restored Julius Nepos as emperor in the West, but his death in AD 480 marked the end of the western empire. The end of the Roman coinage is traditionally placed in AD 498, a date which has no significance for the political history of the empire but was the year in which Anastasius introduced coinage reforms which produced the coinage system of the continuing Byzantine empire.

The coinage produced in both parts of the empire continued frequently to be struck in the names of both the western and eastern emperors, but, because of the complicated political history of the period, it is here set out in two separate sections. The mints situated in the eastern empire mostly continued active, but as the western provinces fell to barbarian conquest the mints there ceased until only the mints in Italy remained active. In this period the importance of Rome as a mint dwindled in comparison with that of Milan, and a new mint at Ravenna.

No great modification took place in the gold denominations of the coinage system, though only the solidus and the tremissis were now produced as regular denominations, with the tremissis playing an increasingly important part. In silver the 'heavy' miliarensis disappeared under Honorius early in the first years of the fifth century, and issues of the 'light' miliarensis became rare. The siliqua in the early fifth century declined in weight to an average of 1.51 gm., and the half-siliqua also diminished in

weight. In bronze the Æ 2 denomination was discontinued about AD 400 and replaced for a time by an improved Æ 3 with an average weight of 2.50 gm., while the Æ 4 which sank to a weight of 1.13 gm. remained the only bronze denomination down to Anastasius' reform of AD 498. In the west, coinage, mostly in gold, produced by the barbarian kingdoms in imitation of and in the names of the legitimate emperors falls outside the scope of this work.

The Western Empire, AD 395–480
Honorius, AD 395–423

1495 Siliqua Trier, AD 420

Obv. D N HONORIVS P F AVG. Bust, pearl-diademed, draped, cuirassed, r.
Rev. VRBS ROMA. Roma seated l. on cuirass, holding Victory on globe, and spear; mint-mark, TRPS. Æ, 1.00 gm. ↑.

A rare coinage was issued for Honorius about AD 420 after the mint of Trier was recovered from the usurper Constantine III.

1496 Solidus Arles, AD 395–408

Obv. As No. 1495.

Rev. VICTORIA AVGGG. Emperor standing r.,
spurning captive with l. foot, holding
standard in r. hand, and Victory on globe
in l.; mint-mark, $\dfrac{\text{A} \mid \text{R}}{\text{COMOB}}$.

N, 4.43 gm. ↑.

The date of this issue as early in the reign is
suggested by the existence of a parallel piece for
Arcadius.

1497 Æ 2 Rome, AD 395–402

Obv. D N ONORIVS P F AVG. Bust, pearl-diademed,
draped, cuirassed, r.
Rev. SALVS REIPVBLICAE. Victory advancing l.,
holding trophy over shoulder with r. hand,
and dragging captive with l.; in field l., ⊬ ;
mint-mark, RT. 1.28 gm. ↓.

This is one of the most common reverses used on the
Æ 4 denomination around the turn of the century.
On the obverse here the silent initial H is omitted
from the name of Honorius.

1498 Solidus Rome, AD 404

Obv. As No. 1495.
Rev. As No. 1496; mint-mark, $\dfrac{\text{R} \mid \text{M}}{\text{COMOB}}$.
N, 4.45 gm. ↓.

This coinage was issued on the occasion of
Honorius' visit to Rome in this year.

1499 Miliarensis Rome, AD 404

Obv. As No. 1495.
Rev. VIRTVS EXERCITVS. Emperor standing r., head
l., holding spear in r. hand, and resting l. on
shield; mint-mark, RMPS. R, 3.81 gm. ↓.
cf. No 1498.

1500 Æ 3 Rome, AD 404

Obv. As No. 1495.
Rev. VRBS ROMA FELIX. Roma standing facing,
holding trophy on spear in r. hand, and
Victory on globe in l.; mint-mark,
$\dfrac{\text{OF} \mid \text{T}}{\text{SMROM}}$.

2.49 gm. ↓.

The period of this Æ 3 coinage is determined by its
issue not only for Honorius but also for Arcadius
and Theodosius II.

1501 Solidus Milan, AD 395–400

Obv. DN HONORIVS P F AVG. Bust, pearl-diademed,
draped, cuirassed, r.
Rev. VICTORIA AVGGG. Emperor standing r.,
spurning captive with l. foot, holding
standard in r. hand, and Victory on globe
in l.; mint-mark, $\dfrac{\text{M} \mid \text{D}}{\text{COMOB}}$.

N, 4.45 gm. ↓.

1502 Half-siliqua Milan, AD 395–400

Obv. As No. 1501.
Rev. VICTORIA AVGGG. Victory advancing l.,
holding wreath in r. hand, and palm-branch
in l.; mint-mark, MD. R, 1.00 gm. ↓.

1503 Solidus Milan, AD 396

Obv. D N HONORIVS P F AVG. Bust, pearl-
    diademed, mantled, l., holding mappa in r.
    hand, and sceptre in l.
Rev. VOTA PVBLICA. Two emperors, nimbate,
    seated facing, enthroned, each holding
    mappa in r. hand, and sceptre in l.;
    below, between emperors, palm-branch;
    mint-mark, $\frac{\text{M} \mid \text{D}}{\text{COMOB}}$.

    N, 4.44 gm. ↑.

A consular solidus issued to mark the joint
consulship of Arcadius and Honorius in AD 396.

1504 Miliarensis Milan, AD 397–8

Obv. D N HONORIVS P F AVG. Bust, pearl-
    diademed, draped, cuirassed, r.
Rev. VOT / V / MVLT / X in wreath; mint-mark,
    MDPS. Æ, 4.31 gm. ↓.

A 'light' miliarensis issued to commemorate
Honorius' quinquennalia.

1505 Solidus Milan, AD 398

Obv. As No. 1503.
Rev. GLORIA ROMANORVM. Emperor, nimbate,
    seated facing, enthroned, holding mappa
    in r. hand, and sceptre in l.; mint-mark,
    $\frac{\text{M} \mid \text{D}}{\text{COMOB}}$.
    N, 4.45 gm. ↓.

1506 Solidus Aquileia, AD 402–3

Obv. As No. 1501.
Rev. As No. 1501; mint-mark, $\frac{\text{A} \mid \text{Q}}{\text{COMOB}}$.

    N, 4.46 gm. ↑.

This coinage was issued at Aquileia between the
cessation of activity at Milan and the opening of the
mint at Ravenna.

1507 Æ 3 Aquileia, AD 408–23

Obv. As No. 1503.
Rev. GLORIA ROMANORVM. Emperor standing
    facing, head r., suppressing captive with r.
    hand, and holding out l. to captive kneeling
    l.; mint-mark, AQS. 1.72 gm. ↑.

The reverse of this Æ 3 denomination was used on
coinage for Honorius only.

1508 Solidus Ravenna, AD 402–3

Obv. As No. 1501.
Rev. As No. 1501, but mint-mark, $\frac{\text{R} \mid \text{V}}{\text{COMOB}}$.

    N, 4.49 gm. ↓.

1509 Semissis Ravenna, AD 402–3

Obv. D N HONORIVS P F AVG. Bust, pearl-
diademed, draped, cuirassed, r.
Rev. VICTORIA AVGVSTORVM. Victory seated r. on
cuirass, inscribing VOT / X / MVLT / XX
on shield supported by Genius; mint-
mark,

$$\frac{\text{R} \mid \text{V}}{\text{COMOB}}.$$

N, 2.23 gm. ↑.

The reverse of this semissis records the vows for
Honorius' decennalia.

1510 Solidus Ravenna, *c.*AD 410

Obv. D N HONORIVS P F AVG. Bust, pearl-
diademed, helmeted, draped, cuirassed, r.
Rev. VICTORIA AVGGG. Emperor standing facing,
crowned by hand of God, holding in r.
hand spear surmounted by ✢, and in l.
sword; beneath right foot, a lion;
mint-mark, $\frac{\text{R} \mid \text{V}}{\text{COB}}$.

N, 4.47 gm. ↓.

1511 Tremissis Ravenna, *c.*AD 410

Obv. D N HONORIVS P F AVG. Bust, pearl-
diademed, draped, cuirassed, r.
Rev. VICTORIA AVGVSTORVM. Victory advancing
r., holding wreath in r. hand, and cross
on globe in l.; mint-mark, $\frac{\text{R} \mid \text{V}}{\text{COM}}$.

N, 1.52 gm. ↑.

1512 Siliqua Ravenna, *c.*AD 410

Obv. As No. 1511.
Rev. VRBS ROMA. Roma seated l., holding Victory
on globe in r. hand, and spear in l.; mint-
mark, RVPS. R, 1.67 gm. ↑.

1513 Solidus Ravenna, *c.*AD 420

Obv. As No. 1511.
Rev. As No. 1501, but mint-mark, $\frac{\text{R} \mid \text{V}}{\text{COMOB}}$.

N, 4.45 gm. ↑.

The style of the obverse portrait, similar to that on
coinage of Constantius III, marks this issue as late in
the reign of Honorius.

1514 Solidus Ravenna, AD 422

Obv. D N HONORIVS P F AVG. Bust facing, pearl-
diademed, mantled, holding mappa in r.
hand, and eagle-tipped sceptre in l.
Rev. VOT XXX MVLT XXX. Emperor seated facing,
enthroned, holding mappa in r. hand, and
eagle-tipped sceptre in l.; mint-mark,

$$\frac{\text{R} \mid \text{V}}{\text{COMOB}}.$$

N, 4.45 gm. ↑.

This consular solidus issued to mark Honorius'
thirteenth consulship in AD 422, at the same time
commemorated the emperor's tricennalia.

1515 Solidus Constantinople, AD 395–402

Obv. D N HONORIVS P F AVG. Bust facing, pearl-
diademed, helmeted, cuirassed, with spear
over shoulder in r. hand, and decorated
shield in l.

Rev. CONCORDIA AVGG. Constantinople seated
facing, head r., r. foot on prow, holding
sceptre in r. hand, and Victory on globe in
l.; mint-mark, CONOB. Ν, 4.47 gm. ↑.

Coinage for Honorius was also struck at mints in the
eastern empire controlled by his brother Arcadius.

1516 Tremissis Constantinople, *c.*AD 410

Obv. D N HONORIVS P F AVG. Bust, pearl-
diademed, draped, cuirassed, r.

Rev. VICTORIA AVGVSTORVM. Victory advancing
r., holding wreath in r. hand, and Victory
on globe in l.; mint-mark, $\frac{| *}{\text{CONOB}}$.

Ν, 1.48 gm. ↑.

1517 Æ 4 Cyzicus, AD 402–8

Obv. As No. 1516.

Rev. CONCORDIA AVGGG. Cross; mint-mark,
SMKA. 1.31 gm. ↓.

The Æ 4 denomination showed a marked
diminution in module.

Constantine III, AD 407–411

1518 Solidus Trier, AD 407–11

Obv. D N CONSTANTINVS P F AVG. Bust, pearl-
diademed, draped, cuirassed, r.

Rev. VICTORIA AVGGG. Emperor standing r.,
holding standard in r. hand, and Victory on
globe in l., spurning captive with l. foot;
mint-mark, TROBS. Ν, 4.57 gm. ↓.

The usurper Constantine III, declared Augustus in
Britain in AD 407, for some years controlled Gaul
and its mints.

1519 Tremissis Arles, AD 407–11

Obv. As No. 1519.

Rev. VICTORIA AVGGG. Victory advancing l.,
holding wreath in r. hand, and globe in
l., mint-mark, $\frac{\text{A | R}}{\text{COMOB}}$.

Ν, 1.26 gm. ↑.

1520 Siliqua Lyons, AD 407–8

Obv. As No. 1519.

Rev. VICTORIA AAAVGGGG. Roma seated l., holding
Victory on globe in r. hand, and spear in l.;
mint-mark, LDPV. Æ, 2.14 gm. ↑.

Priscus Attalus, AD 409–410

1521 Solidus Rome, AD 409–10

Obv. PRISCVS ATTALVS P F AVG. Bust, pearl-diademed, draped, cuirassed, r.
Rev. INVICTA ROMA AETERNA. Roma, seated facing, holding Victory on globe in r. hand, and spear in l.; mint-mark,

$$\frac{R \mid M}{\text{COMOB}}.$$

N, 4.50 gm. ↓.

The Gothic king Alaric, who had seized Rome in AD 409, nominated a puppet emperor Priscus Attalus but deposed him again in AD 410.

1522 Medallion Rome, AD 409–10

Obv. As No. 1522.
Rev. As No. 1522, but mint-mark, RMPS.
Æ, 77.98 gm. ↓.

A silver multiple of 24 siliquae, the equivalent in silver of a solidus.

Jovinus, AD 411–413

1523 Solidus Trier, AD 411–13

Obv. D N IOVINVS P F AVG. Bust, rosette-diademed, draped, cuirassed, r.
Rev. RESTITVTOR REIP. Emperor standing r., holding standard in r. hand, and Victory on globe in l., spurning captive with l. foot; mint-mark,

$$\frac{T \mid R}{\text{COMOB}}.$$

N, 4.47 gm. ↑.

Jovinus, a puppet emperor, set up in Gaul by the Burgundians and Alans, issued coinage from the Gallic mints.

1524 Siliqua Arles, AD 411–13

Obv. As No. 1523, but pearl-diademed.
Rev. RESTITVTOR REIP. Roma seated l., holding Victory on globe in r. hand, and spear in l.; mint-mark, KONT̂. Æ, 3.01 gm. ↑.

Maximus, AD 409–411

1525 Half-siliqua Barcelona, AD 409–11

Obv. D N MAXIMVS P F AVG. Bust, pearl-diademed, draped, cuirassed, r.
Rev. VICTORIA AVGGG. Roma seated l., holding Victory on globe in r. hand, and spear in l.; mint-mark, SMBA. Æ, 0.95 gm. ↓.

Gerontius, the general commanding the troops of Constantine III in Spain, revolted and proclaimed one of his followers, Maximus, emperor.

Constantius III, AD 421

1526 Solidus Ravenna, AD 421

Obv. D N CONSTANTIVS P F AVG. Bust, rosette-
diademed, draped, cuirassed, r.

Rev. VICTORIA AVGGG. Emperor standing r.,
holding standard in r. hand, and Victory
on globe in l., spurning captive with l.
foot; mint-mark, R|V .
N, 4.41 gm. ↓. COMOB

Constantius, who since AD 411 had been virtual
ruler of the western empire, was finally raised by
Honorius to the rank of Augustus in AD 421 but died
shortly afterwards.

Johannes, AD 423–425

1527 Æ 4 Rome, AD 423–5

Obv. D N IOHANNES P F AVG. Bust, pearl-diademed,
draped, cuirassed, r.

Rev. SALVS REIPVBLICE. Victory advancing l.,
holding trophy over shoulder with r. hand,
and dragging captive with l.; in field l., ✚ ;
mint-mark, ЄRM. 1.18 gm. ↓.

The only coinage at the mint of Rome for the brief
reign of Johannes is of the small Æ 4 denomination.

1528 Solidus Ravenna, AD 423–5

Obv. D N IOHANNES P F AVG. Bust, rosette-
diademed, draped, cuirassed, r.

Rev. VICTORIA AVGGG. Emperor standing r.,
holding standard in r. hand, and Victory
on globe in l., spurning captive with l.
foot; mint-mark, R|V .
N, 4.50 gm. ↓. COMOB

1529 Siliqua Ravenna, AD 423–5

Obv. As No. 1528.

Rev. VRBS ROMA. Roma seated l., holding Victory
on globe in r. hand, and spear in l.; mint-
mark, RVPS. Æ, 2.29 gm. ↓.

Valentinian III, AD 425–455

1530 Half-siliqua Trier, AD 425

Obv. D N VALENTINIANVS P F AVG. Bust, pearl-
diademed, draped, cuirassed, r.

Rev. VIRTVS ROMANORVM. Roma seated l.,
holding Victory on globe in r. hand, and
spear in l.; mint-mark, *|___ .
TRPS

Æ, 0.66 gm. ↓.

1531 Solidus Rome, AD 425

Obv. D N PLA VALENTIANVS P F AVG. Bust, pearl-
diademed, draped and cuirassed, r.

Rev. VICTORIA AVGGG. Two emperors standing
facing, each holding long cross in r. hand,
and globe in l., and trampling on
serpent; the emperor on r., is smaller,
and is crowned from heaven; mint-mark,
R|M .
COMOB
N, 4.49 gm. ↓.

Johannes was removed, and Valentinian III made
emperor in the west with the support of his uncle,
Theodosius II, the eastern emperor in AD 425.

1532 Æ 4 Rome, AD 425–6

Obv. As No. 1531.
Rev. SALVS REIPVBLICE. Victory standing l.,
holding wreath in r. hand, and palm-branch
in l.; mint-mark, T̲|̲ .
　　　　　　　　　　RM

0.96 gm. ↓.
This Æ 4 denomination at the outset of the reign
repeated the reverse type used for Johannes.

1533 Æ 4 Rome, *c.*AD 430

Obv. D N VALENTINIANVS P F AVG. Bust, pearl-
diademed, draped, cuirassed, r.
Rev. VICTORIA AVGG. Victory standing l.,
holding wreath in r. hand, and palm-branch
in l.; mint-mark, T̲|̲ .
　　　　　　　　　　RM

1.34 gm. ↓.
Another early Æ 4 denomination used the reverse
type, and form of mint-mark on coins of Honorius
and Theodosius II from the mint of Rome.

1534 Æ 4 Rome, *c.*AD 435

Obv. As No. 1533.
Rev. VOT PVB. Camp-gate; mint-mark, RTM.
Æ, 1.49 gm. ↓.

1535 Solidus Rome, AD 454–5

Obv. LICINIA EVDOXIA P F AVG. Bust with radiate
head-dress surmounted by cross, and with
two long pendants of pearls, draped, facing.

Rev. SALVS REIPVBLICAE. Empress seated
facing enthroned, holding cross on globe
in r. hand, and cross-headed sceptre in
l.; mint-mark, R̲|̲M̲ .
　　　　　　　　COMOB

N, 4.25 gm. ↑.
Coinage by Valentinian III for Licinia Eudoxia, the
daughter of Theodosius II whom he married in
AD 437 (cf. also Nᵒ. 1546).

1536 Solidus Rome, AD 455

Obv. D N PLA VALENTINIANVS P F AVG. Bust,
rosette-diademed, mantled l., holding
mappa in r. hand, and cross-headed sceptre
in l.
Rev. VOT XXX MVLT XXXX. Emperor standing
facing in consular robes, holding cross-
headed sceptre in l. hand, with r. hand
raising kneeling female figure;
mint-mark, R̲|̲M̲ .
　　　　　　　COMOB

N, 4.44 gm. ↑.
Solidus issued to commemorate Valentinian III's
eighth consulship in AD 455.

1537 Solidus Ravenna, AD 425-30

Obv. D N GALLA PLACIDIA P F AVG. Bust, pearl-
diademed, draped, r., with Chi-Rho on
shoulder, and above, hand of God.
Rev. VOT XX MVLT XXX. Victory standing l.,
holding long cross;.mint-mark, R̲|̲V̲ .
　　　　　　　　　　　　COMOB

N, 4.47 gm. ↓.
Coinage for Galla Placidia, widow of Constantius
III and mother of Valentinian III, issued after the
latter became western emperor in AD 425.

1538 Solidus Ravenna, c.AD 430

Obv. D N PLA VALENTINIANVS P F AVG. Bust, rosette-diademed, draped, cuirassed, r.
Rev. VICTORIA AVGGG. Emperor standing facing, holding long cross-headed sceptre in r. hand, and Victory on globe in l., r. foot on head of human-headed serpent; mint-mark, $\frac{R \mid V}{COMOB}$. ᴀ́, 4.46 gm. ↓.

1539 Half-siliqua Ravenna, AD 430–40

Obv. As No. 1540.
Rev. Chi-Rho in wreath; mint-mark, RV. ᴁ, 0.85 gm. ↓.

1540 Solidus Ravenna, c.AD 435

Obv. D N IVST GRAT HONORIA P F AVG. Bust, pearl-diademed, draped, r., with cross on shoulder, and above head, hand of God.
Rev. BONO REIPVBLICAE. Victory standing l., holding long cross; mint-mark, $\frac{R \mid V}{COMOB}$. ᴀ́, 4.39 gm. ↓.
Coinage by Valentinian III for his sister, Honoria, to whom he gave the rank of Augusta.

1541 Siliqua Ravenna, AD 440–50

Obv. As No. 1538, but pearl-diademed and rosette on shoulder.
Rev. VRBS ROMA. Roma seated l., holding Victory on globe in r. hand, and spear in l.; mint-mark, RVPS. ᴁ, 2.00 gm. ↑.

1542 Siliqua Ravenna, AD 440–50

Obv. As No. 1537, but rosette on shoulder, and no hand of God.
Rev. SALVS REIPVBLICAE. Victory seated r. on cuirass inscribing Chi-Rho on shield held on knee; mint-mark, RVPS. ᴁ, 2.18 gm. ↓.

1543 Half-siliqua Ravenna, AD 430–40

Obv. As No. 1542.
Rev. Chi-Rho in wreath; mint-mark, RV. ᴁ, 0.88 gm. ↓.

1544 Solidus Constantinople, AD 425–6

Obv. D N VALENTINIANVS P F AVG. Bust, diademed, helmeted, cuirassed, facing, holding spear over shoulder in r. hand, and decorated shield in l.
Rev. SALVS REIPVBLICAE Z. Two emperors, nimbate, seated facing, enthroned, each holding mappa in r. hand, and globe in l.; above, star; mint-mark, CONOB. ᴀ́, 4.37 gm. ↓.
The two emperors on the reverse are Theodosius and Valentinian III, the latter shown as a much smaller figure, emphasising both his age and his junior status.

1545 Siliqua Constantinople, AD 425–6

Obv. D N VALENTINIANVS P F AVG. Bust, pearl-diademed, draped, cuirassed, r.
Rev. VOT / XX / MVLT / XXX in wreath; mint-mark, CONS✱. Æ, 2.06 gm. ↓.

The reverse records Valentinian III's vicennalian vota in the year AD 425.

1546 Solidus Constantinople, AD 443

Obv. AEL EVDOXIA AVG. Bust, pearl-diademed, draped, r.; above, hand of God.
Rev. IMP XXXXII COS XVII P P. Constantinopolis seated l., r. foot on prow, holding cross on globe in r. hand, and sceptre in l.; mint-mark, ✱| / CONOB .
Æ, 4.22 gm. ↓.

Eudoxia, the wife of Valentinian III (cf. No. 1535) shared in the coinage issued by her father, Theodosius II, at Constantinople.

Petronius Maximus, AD 455

1547 Solidus Rome, AD 455

Obv. D N PETRONIVS MAXIMVS P F AVG. Bust, pearl-diademed, draped, cuirassed, r.
Rev. VICTORIA AVGGG. Emperor standing facing, holding long cross-headed sceptre in r. hand, and Victory on globe in l., placing r. foot on head of human-headed serpent; mint-mark, R|M / COMOB .
Æ, 4.50 gm. ↓.

The murder of Valentinian III was procured by the senator Maximus who succeeded him as emperor, but after a reign of only some seventy days he was killed when the Vandals under Gaiseric sacked Rome.

Avitus, AD 455–456

1548 Solidus Arles, AD 455–6

Obv. D N AVITVS PERP F AVG. Bust, rosette-diademed, draped, cuirassed, r.
Rev. VICTORIA AVGGG. Emperor standing facing, head r., holding long cross-headed sceptre in r. hand, and Victory on globe in l., spurning captive with l. foot; mint-mark, A|R / COMOB .
Æ, 4.41 gm. ↓.

On the death of Petronius Maximus, Avitus, a Gallo-Roman noble, was proclaimed emperor with the backing of the Visigothic king Thorismund, but was deposed in AD 456 by the patrician Ricimer.

Majorian, AD 457–461

1549 Solidus Ravenna, AD 458

Obv. D N IVLIVS MAIORIANVS P F AVG. Bust, pearl-diademed, facing, mantled, holding mappa in r. hand and cross-headed sceptre in l.
Rev. VOTIS MVLTIS. Two emperors, nimbate, seated facing, each holding mappa in r. hand, and cross-headed sceptre in l.; mint-mark, R|V / COMOB .
Æ, 4.35 gm. ↓.

After a brief interregnum following the death of Avitus Majorian was declared emperor, but after a few years he aroused the jealousy of the powerful

Ricimer, and was seized and killed at Tortona in AD 461. The consular representation dates the coin to Majorian's consulship in AD 458. On the reverse, the emperor accompanying Majorian is the eastern emperor Leo I.

1550 Solidus Arles, AD 457–61

Obv. D N IVLIVS MAIORIANVS P F AVG. Bust, rosette-diademed, helmeted, cuirassed, r., with spear in r. hand, and shield in l.
Rev. VICTORIA AVGGG. Emperor standing facing, holding long cross-headed sceptre in r. hand, and Victory on globe in l., placing r. foot on human-headed serpent; mint-mark, $\frac{\text{A} \mid \text{R}}{\text{COMOB}}$.
N, 4.48 gm. ↓.

1551 Æ 4 Milan, AD 457–61

Obv. D N IVL MAIORIANVS P F AVG. Bust, pearl-diademed, draped, cuirassed, r.
Rev. VICTORIA AVGGG. Victory standing l., holding wreath in r. hand, and palm-branch in l.; mint-mark, MD. 1.21 gm. ↓.
The reign of Majorian is one of only two occasions when bronze coinage was struck at the mint of Milan.

Libius Severus, AD 461–465

1552 Solidus Rome, AD 461–5

Obv. D N LIBIVS SEVERVS P F AVG. Bust, pearl-diademed, draped, cuirassed, r.
Rev. VICTORIA AVGGG. Emperor standing facing, holding long cross-headed sceptre

in r. hand, and Victory on globe in l., placing r. foot on human-headed serpent; mint-mark, $\frac{\text{R} \mid \text{M}}{\text{COMOB}}$.
N, 4.44 gm. ↓.
Ricimer replaced Majorian with a new puppet emperor, Libius Severus.

1553 Semissis Rome, AD 461–5

Obv. As No. 1552, but rosette-diademed.
Rev. SALVS REIPVBLICAE. Chi-Rho in wreath; mint-mark, COMOB. *N*, 2.19 gm. ↓.

1554 Half-siliqua Rome, AD 461–5

Obv. D N LIB SEVERVS P F AVG. Bust, pearl-diademed, draped, cuirassed, r.
Rev. Chi-Rho in wreath; mint-mark, RM. *R*, 0.91 gm. ↑.

1555 Æ 4 Rome, AD 461–5

Obv. As No. 1554.
Rev. Monogram R⅍E 0.81 gm. ↓.
The monogram on the reverse of this Æ 4 denomination is that of the patrician Ricimer.

1556 Solidus Milan, AD 461–5

Obv. As No. 1552, but PE instead of PF and rosette-diademed.
Rev. As No. 1552, but mint-mark, $\frac{\text{M} \mid \text{D}}{\text{COMOB}}$.
N, 4.42 gm. ↑.

Anthemius, AD 467–472

1557 Solidus Rome, AD 467–72

Obv. D N ANTHEMIVS P F AVG. Bust, pearl-
diademed, helmeted, cuirassed, facing,
holding spear over shoulder in r. hand, and
shield in l.

Rev. SALVS REIPVBLICAE. Leo I and Anthemius
standing facing, holding spears, and together
holding cross on globe; mint-mark,

$$\frac{*}{\text{CORMOB}}$$

N, 4.43 gm. ↓.

After an interregnum of two years when the empire
was nominally united under the eastern emperor
Leo I, Anthemius, son-in-law of the late eastern
emperor Marcian, was created Augustus of the
west, but in his turn was overthrown by Ricimer.

1558 Half-siliqua Rome, AD 467–72

Obv. D N ANTHEMIVS PERPET AVG. Bust, pearl-
diademed, draped, cuirassed, r.

Rev. Chi-Rho in wreath; mint-mark, RM.
Æ, 0.87 gm. ↑.

1559 Æ 4 Rome, AD 467–72

Obv. D N ANTHEMIVS P F AVG. Bust, pearl-
diademed, draped, cuirassed, r.

Rev. Monogram ₳; mint-mark, RM. 1.79 gm. ↑.
On late Æ 4 denominations the most usual reverse is
that of a monogram of the emperor's name.

1560 Solidus Rome, AD 467–72

Obv. D N AEL MARC EVFEMIAE P P AVG. Bust,
diademed, draped, r.

Rev. VICTORIA AVGGG *. Victory standing l.,
holding long cross; mint-mark, CORMOB.
N, 4.40 gm. ↓.

Coinage was struck for the empress Eufemia,
daughter of the late eastern emperor Marcian. The
mint initial R is here unusually incorporated into the
middle of the formula COMOB, as on No. 1557.

Olybrius, AD 472

1561 Solidus Rome, AD 472

Obv. D N ANICIVS OLYBRIVS AVG. Bust, pearl-
diademed, draped, cuirassed, facing.

Rev. SALVS MVNDI. Cross; mint-mark, COMOB.
N, 4.37 gm. ↓.

Olybrius, sent by Leo to aid Anthemius against
Ricimer, was prevailed on by Ricimer to be
nominated emperor before the overthrow of
Anthemius. The reverse type is one of the most
specifically Christian on the late Roman coinage.

Glycerius, AD 473-474

1562 Solidus Ravenna, AD 473-4

Obv. D N GLYCERIVS F P AVG. Bust, rosette-
diademed, draped, cuirassed, r.

Rev. VICTORIA AVGGG. Emperor standing
facing, holding long cross-headed sceptre
in r. hand, and Victory on globe in l.,
placing l. foot on step; mint-mark,

$$\frac{\text{R} \mid \text{V}}{\text{COMOB}}.$$

Ν, 4.43 gm. ↓.

On Ricimer's death his position of influence was
taken over by his nephew Gundobad, with whose
support Glycerius proclaimed himself emperor.
The style of this coin is notably archaistic, both in its
obverse, reminiscent of the style of the mid-fourth
century, and in its reverse which revives a common
type of Honorius.

Julius Nepos, AD 474-475

1563 Solidus Arles, AD 474-5

Obv. D N IVL NEPOS P F AVG. Bust, pearl-diademed,
helmeted, cuirassed, facing, holding spear
over shoulder on r. hand, and shield in l.

Rev. VICTORIA AVGGG. Victory standing l.,
holding long cross; mint-mark, $\frac{\text{A} \mid \text{R}}{\text{COMOB}}$.

Ν, 4.35 gm. ↓.

Glycerius had not been recognised by the eastern
emperor Leo I, who had Nepos proclaimed western
emperor. The deposed Glycerius was made bishop
of Salonae in Dalmatia.

1564 Tremissis Milan, AD 474-5

Obv. D N IVL NEPOS P F AVG. Bust, pearl-diademed,
draped, cuirassed r.

Rev. Cross in wreath; mint-mark, COMOB.
Ν, 1.46 gm. ↓.

1565 Solidus Ravenna, AD 474-5

Obv. As No. 1563.

Rev. As No. 1563, but VICTORIA AVGGG:, and
mint-mark, $\frac{\text{R} \mid \text{V}}{\text{COMOB}}$.

Ν, 4.4 gm. ↓.

1566 Siliqua Ravenna, AD 474-5

Obv. As No. 1564

Rev. VRBIS ROMA. Roma seated facing, head
l., holding Victory on globe in
r. hand, and sceptre in l.; mint-mark, RVPS.
Ρ, 1.97 gm. ↓.

1567 Half-siliqua Ravenna, AD 474-5

Obv. As No. 1564.

Rev. Turreted figure standing l., r. foot on prow,
holding staff in r. hand, and cornucopiae in
l.; mint-mark, RV. Ρ, 0.86 gm. ↑.

Romulus Augustus, AD 475–476

1568 Solidus Milan, AD 475–6

Obv. D N ROMVLVS AGVSTVS P F AVG. Bust, pearl-diademed, helmeted, cuirassed, facing, holding spear over shoulder in r. hand, and shield in l.
Rev. VICTORIA AVGGG. Victory standing l., holding long cross, mint-mark, $\underline{\quad | *}$.
COMOB

N, 4.41 gm. ↑.

Orestes, appointed *magister militim* by Nepos in AD 475, turned against the emperor who was compelled to flee to Dalmatia, and Orestes proclaimed his young son Romulus emperor. After only a year he was deposed by Odovacar, king of the German tribes in Italy. Odovacar did not set up a new puppet emperor, but offered recognition of the eastern emperor Zeno in return for recognition as patrician and ruler of Italy.

Julius Nepos (restored), AD 476–480

1569 Solidus Milan, AD 476–80

Obv. D N IVL NEPOS P F AVG. Bust, pearl-diademed, helmeted, cuirassed, facing, holding spear over shoulder in r. hand, and shield in l.
Rev. VICTORIA AVGGG. Victory standing l., holding long cross; mint-mark, $\underline{\quad M | D}$.
COMOB

N, 4.29 gm. ↓.

Odovacar's recognition of Zeno ensured acceptance of Julius Nepos as still nominal western emperor at least, and coins were struck at the Italian mints in the name of Nepos down to his assassination in AD 480.

The Eastern Empire, AD 395–498

Arcadius, AD 395–408

1570 Miliarensis Rome, AD 404

Obv. D N ARCADIVS P F AVG. Bust, pearl-diademed, draped, cuirassed, r.
Rev. VIRTVS EXERCITVS. Emperor standing facing, head l., holding spear in r. hand and resting l. hand on shield; mint-mark, RMPS.

AR, 4.33 gm. ↑.

A miliarensis of the 'light' standard of the joint reign of Arcadius and Honorius.

1571 Siliqua Rome, *c*.AD 404

Obv. As No. 1570.
Rev. VIRTVS ROMANORVM. Roma seated l. on cuirass holding Victory on globe in r. hand, and spear in l.; mint-mark, RMPS.

AR, 1.29 gm. ↑.

1572 Solidus Ravenna, *c*.AD 408

Obv. As No. 1570.
Rev. VICTORIA AVGGG. Emperor standing r., holding standard in r. hand, and Victory on globe in l., spurning captive with l. foot; mint-mark, $\underline{\quad R | V}$.
COMOB

N, 4.50 gm. ↓.

1573 Solidus Milan, AD 397–8

Obv. D N ARCADIVS P F AVG. Bust, pearl-diademed,
helmeted, cuirassed, facing, holding spear
over shoulder in r. hand, and shield in l.
Rev. VOTA PLVRIA. Two emperors, nimbate,
seated facing, together holding shield
surmounted by cross, and inscribed VOT / XV
/ MVLT / XX; below, between emperors,
palm-branch; mint-mark, COMOB.
𝒩, 4.53 gm. ↑.

The reverse presents a unique form of vota
inscription. The vota recorded on the shield are
those for Arcadius' quindecennalia in AD 397–8.

1574 Solidus Constantinople, AD 396–401

Obv. As No. 1573.
Rev. CONCORDIA AVGG Γ. Constantinopolis seated
facing, head r., holding sceptre in r. hand,
and Victory on globe in r., r. foot on prow;
mint-mark, CONOB. 𝒩, 4.46 gm. ↓.

The reverse inscription indicates that the issue falls
in the period of the two emperors Arcadius and
Honorius, before the proclamation of Theodosius II.
The officina letter is appended to the reverse inscription.

1575 Solidus Constantinople, AD 400

Obv. AEL EVDOXIA AVG. Bust, diademed, draped
r., above head, hand of God.
Rev. SALVS REIPVBLICAE. Victory seated r. on
cuirass, inscribing Chi-Rho on shield set on
column; mint-mark, CONOB. 𝒩, 4.44 gm. ↓.
Arcadius proclaimed his empress, Eudoxia, Augusta
in AD 400.

1576 Tremissis Constantinople, AD 400

Obv. As No. 1575, but without hand.
Rev. Cross in wreath; mint-mark, CON.
𝒩, 1.47 gm. ↑.

1577 Æ 3 Constantinople, AD 402

Obv. As No. 1575.
Rev. As No. 1575, but mint-mark, CONSA.
Æ, 1.85 gm. ↑.

1578 Solidus Constantinople, AD 404–5

Obv. D N ARCADIVS P F AVG. Bust, pearl-diademed,
helmeted, cuirassed, facing, holding spear
over shoulder in r. hand, and shield in l.
Rev. NOVA SPES REIPVBLICAE. Victory seated
r. on cuirass, inscribing XX / XXX on shield
held on knee; mint-mark, $\frac{* |}{\text{CONOB}}$.

𝒩, 4.50 gm. ↓.

The hope for the future expressed by the reverse
inscription refers to the proclamation by Arcadius
in AD 402 of his infant son Theodosius II as Augustus
and to his own twentieth anniversary.

1579 Æ 3 Nicomedia, AD 402

Obv. As No. 1578.
Rev. CONCORDIA AVGG. Constantinopolis seated
facing, head r., holding sceptre in r. hand,
and Victory on globe in l., r. foot on prow;
mint-mark, SMNA. 2.29 gm. ↑.
The Æ 3 denomination of this period was slightly
improved in module and weight.

1580 Æ 3 Cyzicus, AD 395–400

Obv. D N ARCADIVS P F AVG. Bust, pearl-diademed,
draped, cuirassed, r.
Rev. VIRTVS EXERCITI. Emperor standing facing,
head r., holding spear in r. hand, and resting
l. on shield, crowned with wreath by
Victory standing l., holding palm branch in
l. hand; mint-mark, SMKB. 2.49 gm. ↓.

Theodosius II, AD 402–450

1581 Siliqua Trier, AD 425

Obv. D N THEODOSIVS P F AVG. Bust, pearl-
diademed, draped, cuirassed, r.
Rev. VRTVS ROMANORVM. Roma seated l., holding
Victory on globe in r. hand and spear in
l.; mint-mark, ＊| .
                   TRPS
  Æ, 0.96 gm. ↑.
This coin represents the latest coinage which was
struck at Trier for an eastern emperor.

1582 Solidus Aquileia, AD 425

Obv. D N THEODOSIVS P F AVG. Bust, pearl-
diademed, helmeted, cuirassed, facing, holding
spear over shoulder in r. hand, and shield in l.
Rev. SALVS REIPVBLICAE. Theodosius II seated
facing in consular robes, holding mappa
in r. hand, and cross in l.; to his left,
Valentinian III standing facing, holding
mappa in r. hand, and cross in l.; above,
star; mint-mark, A | Q .
                    COMOB
  Ν, 4.48 gm. ↓.
The consular figures of Theodosius II and
Valentinian III Caesar on the reverse mark their joint
consulship in AD 425.

1583 Solidus Ravenna, AD 423–5

Obv. D N THEODOSIVS P F AVG. Bust, pearl-
diademed, draped, cuirassed, r.
Rev. VICTORIA AVGGG. Emperor standing r.,
holding standard in r. hand, and Victory
on globe in l. spurning captive with l.
foot; mint-mark, R | V .
                    COMOB
  Ν, 4.48 gm. ↓.
This coinage was issued during the reign of the
western emperor Johannes, though Theodosius II
did not extend recognition to him.

1584 Solidus Thessalonica, AD 402–4

Obv. D N THEODOSIVS P F AVG. Bust, pearl-
diademed, helmeted, cuirassed, facing, holding
spear over shoulder in r. hand, and shield in l.

Rev. CONCORDIA AVGGG. Constantinopolis seated
facing, head r., holding sceptre in r. hand,
and Victory on globe in l., r. foot on prow;
mint-mark, COMOB. Æ, 4.36 gm. ↑.

1585 Solidus Thessalonica, AD 424–5

Obv. As No. 1584.
Rev. GLOR ORVIS TERRAR. Emperor standing
facing, holding standard in r. hand, and
cross in l.; mint-mark, $\frac{*|}{\text{TESOB}}$.

Æ, 4.29 gm. ↓.
On this new reverse type the word *orbis* is
consistently spelled *orvis*. This coinage was issued
when Theodosius II was sole Augustus, between
the death of Honorius and the nomination of
Valentinian III.

1586 Solidus Constantinople, AD 402

Obv. As No. 1584.
Rev. CONCORDIA AVGGG. Constantinopolis seated
facing, head r., holding sceptre in r. hand,
and Victory on globe in l., r. foot on prow;
mint-mark, CONOB. Æ, 4.36 gm. ↓.
That this is an early coin of Theodosius is apparent
both from the small, narrow bust on obverse, but
also from the fact that the reverse die, originally for
coinage for Arcadius and Honorius and ending
AVGGS (S = officina 6) has been altered to read
AVGGG.

1587 Solidus Constantinople, AD 408–20

Obv. D N THEODOSIVS P F AVG. Bust, helmeted,
cuirassed, facing, holding spear over
shoulder in r. hand, and shield in l.
Rev. CONCORDIA AVGGGI. Constantinopolis
seated facing, head r., holding sceptre
in r. hand, and Victory on globe in l.,
r. foot on prow; mint-mark, $\frac{*|}{\text{CONOB}}$.

Æ, 4.43 gm. ↓.
An issue of the joint reign of Honorius and
Theodosius II. At the end of the reverse inscription is
the officina number $I = 10$.

1588 Miliarensis Constantinople, *c.*AD 410

Obv. D N THEODOSIVS P F AVG. Bust, pearl-
diademed, draped, cuirassed, l.
Rev. GLORIA ROMANORVM. Emperor, nimbate,
standing facing, head l., raising r.
hand, and holding globe in l.;
mint-mark, $\frac{*|}{\text{CON}}$.

Æ, 4.29 gm. ↑.

1589 Solidus Constantinople, AD 415

Obv. D N THEODOSIVS P F AVG. Bust, pearl-
diademed, helmeted, draped, cuirassed, r.,
holding spear and shield.
Rev. GLORIA REIPVBLICAE. Roma head r., and
Constantinopolis head l., seated facing,
holding sceptre in l. and r. hand
respectively, together holding shield
inscribed VOT / XV / MVL / XX;
Constantinopolis places r. foot
on prow; mint-mark, $\frac{*|}{\text{CONOB}}$.

Æ, 4.49 gm. ↓.

1590 Solidus Constantinople, AD 415–20

Obv. AEL PVLCHERIA AVG. Bust, diademed, draped
r.; above, hand of God.

Rev. SALVS REIPVBLICAE. Victory seated r.
on cuirass, inscribing Chi-Rho on shield
held on knee; mint-mark, ___*_|___ .
                           CONOB

N, 4.44 gm. ↓.

Pulcheria, sister of Theodosius II, exercised great
influence on her brother throughout his reign. She
was proclaimed Augusta in AD 414.

1591 Siliqua Constantinople, AD 415–20

Obv. As No. 1590, but no hand.

Rev. Cross in wreath; mint-mark, CONS*.

    AR, 1.76 gm. ↑.

1592 Solidus Constantinople, AD 420

Obv. D N THEODOSIVS P F AVG. Bust, pearl-
diademed, mantled, l., holding mappa in r.
hand, and cross-headed sceptre in l.

Rev. VOT XX MVLT XXX. Victory standing l.,
holding long cross; mint-mark, CONOB.

    N, 4.46 gm. ↑.

The obverse shows Theodosius II in consular dress
on the occasion of his tenth consulship. The reverse
recording the emperor's vicennalia is the first
representation of Victory holding a long cross, a
type used to honour a victory over the Persians to
relieve persecution of the Christians.

1593 Tremissis Constantinople, AD 421–2

Obv. D N THEODOSIVS P F AVG. Bust, pearl-
diademed and draped, cuirassed, r.

Rev. Trophy; mint-mark, ___*_|_*___ .
                         CONOB

    N, 1.48 gm. ↓.

The reverse type relates the coin to the Persian wars
of AD 421–2.

1594 Solidus Constantinople, AD 423

Obv. AEL EVDOCIA AVG. Bust, diademed, draped,
r.; above, hand of God.

Rev. As No. 1592. N, 4.48 gm. ↓.

Coinage was issued in AD 422 in honour of Eudocia
whom Theodosius II married in AD 421, and
proclaimed Augusta in AD 423.

1595 Solidus Constantinople, AD 424–5

Obv. D N THEODOSIVS P F AVG. Bust, pearl-
diademed, helmeted, cuirassed, facing,
holding spear over shoulder in r. hand, and
shield in l.

Rev. GLOR ORVIS TERRAR. Emperor, helmeted,
standing facing holding standard in
r. hand, and cross on globe in l.;
mint-mark, ___*_|___ .
                    CONOB

    N, 4.48 gm. ↑.

A parallel issue at this mint to No. 1585.

1596 Solidus Constantinople, AD 425

Obv. As No. 1595.

Rev. SALVS REIPVBLICAE. Theodosius II seated facing in consular dress, holding mappa in r. hand, and cross in l.; to his left, Valentinian III standing facing in consular dress, holding mappa in r. hand, and cross in l.; above, star; mint-mark, CONOB. N, 4.38 gm. ↓.

A parallel issue at this mint to No. 1582.

1597 Æ 4 Constantinople, AD 425–30

Obv. D N THEODOSIVS P F AVG. Bust, pearl-diademed, draped, cuirassed, r.

Rev. CONCORDIA AVG. Victory standing facing holding wreath in each hand; mint-mark, CON. 1.17 gm. ↑.

1598 Siliqua Constantinople, AD 430

Obv. AEL EVDOCIA AVG. Bust, diademed, draped, r.

Rev. Cross in wreath; mint-mark, CONS*. Æ, 1.74 gm. ↓.

1599 Solidus Constantinople, AD 430

Obv. D N THEODOSIVS P F AVG. Bust, pearl-diademed, mantled, l.; holding mappa in r. hand, and cross-headed sceptre in l.

Rev. VOT XXX MVLT XXXX. As No. 1595, but emperors nimbate, and both seated; mint-mark, CONOB. N, 4.32 gm. ↓.

A 'consular' solidus issued for the joint consulship in AD 430 when Theodosius II was consul for the thirteenth time, and Valentinian III for the third time.

1600 Semissis Constantinople, AD 430 or 435

Obv. D N THEODOSIVS P F AVG. Bust, pearl-diademed, draped, cuirassed, r.

Rev. VICTORIA AVGG. Victory seated r. on cuirass, inscribing XXXV on shield held on knee; mint-mark, $\frac{* \mid +}{\text{CONOB}}$.

N, 2.15 gm. ↓.

The correct date depends on whether the vota here are to be regarded as *soluta* or *suscepta*.

1601 Solidus Constantinople, AD 430–9

Obv. As No. 1595.

Rev. VOT XXX MVLT XXXX. Roma seated l., shield by side, holding cross on globe in r. hand, and sceptre in l.; mint-mark, $\frac{\mid *}{\text{CONOB}}$.

N, 4.46 gm. ↓.

1602 Siliqua Constantinople, AD 435–40

Obv. As No. 1600.

Rev. Within wreath VOT / MVLT / XXXX; mint-mark, CONS*. Æ, 4.42 gm. ↑.

1603 Solidus Constantinople, AD 437

Obv. As No. 1595.
Rev. FELICITER NVBTIIS. Theodosius II, nimbate, standing facing, placing hand on shoulder of Valentinian III, nimbate, standing facing on his r., and of Licinia Eudoxia, nimbate, standing facing on his l.; Valentinian III and Licinia Eudoxia join hands; mint-mark, CONOB. N, 4.47 gm. ↓.

The reverse commemorates the marriage of Theodosius II's daughter Licinia Eudoxia to Valentinian III in AD 437.

1604 Solidus Constantinople, AD 440

Obv. As No. 1595.
Rev. VIRT EXERC ROM. Virtus advancing r., dragging captive with r. hand, and holding trophy over shoulder in l.; mint-mark, $\frac{|\ *}{\text{CONOB}}$.
N, 4.45 gm. ↓.

1605 Solidus Constantinople, AD 443

Obv. As No. 1595.
Rev. IMP XXXXII COS XVII PP. Constantinopolis seated l., shield by side, holding cross on globe in r. hand and sceptre in l.; foot on prow; mint-mark, $\frac{*\ |}{\text{COMOB}}$.
N, 4.48 gm. ↓.

The absence of officina number and the reading COMOB and not CONOB suggests that this coinage

was not issued at Constantinople, but a travelling mint accompanying Theodosius II on his travels in AD 443, the *expeditio Asiana*.

1606 Æ 2 Constantinople, AD 440–50

Obv. D N THEODOSIVS P F AVG. Bust, helmeted, pearl-diademed, cuirassed and bearded, r., with spear and shield.
Rev. CONCORDIA AGV. Two emperors, nimbate, standing facing, holding spears in r. and l. hands respectively, and supporting between them a long cross; mint-mark, CONS. Æ, 4.13 gm. ↓.

The Æ 2 denomination was revived in this coinage. These bronzes appear to have had wide currency in the Crimea, and appear commonly in finds from Cherson (cf. also Nos. 1624–5).

1607 Æ 4 Cyzicus, AD 402–8

Obv. As No. 1600, but star in field l.
Rev. GLORIA ROMANORVM. Three emperors standing facing; centre figure is smaller and holds spear in r. hand; emperor on l. holds spear in r. hand and rests l. on shield; emperor on r. rests r. hand on shield and holds spear in l.; mint-mark, SMKA. 1.79 gm. ↓.

The small figure in centre on the reverse is the young Theodosius II, flanked by his father Arcadius, and his uncle Honorius.

1608 Æ 4 Cyzicus, AD 408–23

Obv. As No. 1607.

Rev. GLORIA ROMANORVM. Two emperors standing facing, each holding spear and resting hand on shield; mint-mark, SMKΔ. 1.92 gm. ↑.

The two emperors here are Honorius and Theodosius II.

1609 Æ **4** Alexandria, AD 402–8

Obv. As No. 1600.
Rev. CONCORDIA AVGGG. Cross; mint-mark, ALEA. 1.51 gm. ↑.

Marcian, AD 450–457

1610 Solidus Ravenna, AD 456–7

Obv. D N MARCIANVS P F AVG. Bust, rosette-diademed, draped, cuirassed, r.
Rev. VICTORIA AVGGG. Emperor standing facing, holding long cross in r. hand, and Victory on globe in l., r. foot on head of human-headed serpent; mint-mark,

$$\frac{R \mid V}{\text{CONOB}}.$$

N, 4.38 gm. ↓.

1611 Solidus Thessalonica, AD 450–7

Obv. D N MARCIANVS P F AVG. Bust, pearl-diademed, helmeted, cuirassed, facing, holding spear over shoulder in r. hand, and shield in l.
Rev. GLOR ORVIS TERRAR. Emperor standing facing, holding long cross in r. hand, and cross on globe in l.; mint-mark, $\dfrac{* \mid}{\text{TESOB}}$.

N, 4.28 gm. ↓.

1612 Solidus Constantinople, AD 450–7

Obv. As No. 1611.
Rev. VICTORIA AVGGGA. Victory standing facing, head l., holding long cross in r. hand; mint-mark, $\dfrac{\mid *}{\text{COMOB}}$.

N, 4.43 gm. ↓.

1613 Tremissis Constantinople, AD 450–7

Obv. D N MARCIANVS P F AVG. Bust, pearl-diademed, draped, cuirassed, r.
Rev. VICTORIA AVGVSTORVM. Victory advancing l., holding wreath in r. hand, and cross on globe in l.; mint-mark, $\dfrac{\mid *}{\text{CONOB}}$.

N, 1.50 gm. ↑.

1614 Miliarensis Constantinople, AD 450–7

Obv. As No. 1613, but emperor bearded.
Rev. GLORIA ROMANORVM. Emperor, nimbate, standing facing, head l., holding spear in r. hand, and resting l. on shield; mint-mark, $\dfrac{* \mid}{\text{CON}}$.

Æ, 5.15 gm. ↓.

1615 Siliqua Constantinople, AD 450–7

Obv. As No. 1613.
Rev. SAL / REI / PVI / in wreath; mint-mark,
CONS*. Æ, 1.54 gm. ↓.

1616 Æ 4 Constantinople, AD 450–7

Obv. As No. 1613.
Rev. Within wreath, monogram ℞; mint-mark, CON. 1.39 gm. ↑.

1617 Solidus Constantinople, AD 450–57

Obv. AEL PVLCHERIA AVG. Bust, diademed, draped, r.
Rev. VICTORIA AVGGG. Victory standing l., holding long cross; mint-mark,

$$\frac{\quad | * \quad}{\text{CONOB}}.$$

Æ, 4.43 gm. ↓.
After the death of Theodosius II, Pulcheria married his successor, Marcian.

Leo I, AD 457–474

1618 Solidus Rome, AD 465–7

Obv. D N LEO PERPETVVS AVG. Bust, rosette-diademed, draped, cuirassed, r.

Rev. VICTORIA AVGGG. Emperor, standing facing, holding long cross in r. hand, and Victory on globe in l., r. foot on head of human-headed serpent; mint-mark,

$$\frac{\text{R} | \text{M}}{\text{COMOB}}.$$

Æ, 4.34 gm. ↓.
This coinage formed part of an issue struck at Rome probably in the interregnum between Libius Severus and Anthemius.

1619 Solidus Thessalonica, AD 457–474

Obv. D N LEO PERPET AVG. Bust, pearl-diademed, mantled, l., holding mappa in r. hand, and cross in l.
Rev. VICTORIA AVGGG. Emperor, nimbate, seated facing, in consular dress, holding mappa in r. hand, and cross in l.; mint-mark,

$$\frac{\quad * | \quad}{\text{THSOB}}.$$

Æ, 4.44 gm. ↓.
It is not possible to determine on which of several consular years Leo was in Thessalonica. Though the obverse style is that of Thessalonica, the style of the reverse resembles that used by die engravers at Constantinople.

1620 Solidus Thessalonica, *c.* AD 470

Obv. D N LEO PERPET AVG. Bust, pearl-diademed, helmeted, cuirassed, facing, holding spear over shoulder in r. hand, and shield in l.
Rev. VICTORIA AVGGG. Victory standing l., holding long cross in r. hand; mint-mark,

$$\frac{\quad * | * \quad}{\text{THSOB}}.$$

Æ, 4.45 gm. ↓.
The use of the double star in the mint-mark seems to be later than the single star as used on No. 1619.

1621 Miliarensis Thessalonica, AD 457–474

Obv. D N LEO PERPET AVG. Bust, pearl-diademed, draped, cuirassed, r.

Rev. GLOR ORVS TERRRHL. Emperor, nimbate, standing facing, holding spear in r. hand, and resting l. on shield; mint-mark,

　　＊│
　　THSOB

Æ, 4.53 gm. ↓.

By this period the original significance of the letters OB, meaning pure gold had been forgotten. The reverse inscription has been badly blundered.

1622 Solidus Constantinople, *c.*AD 460

Obv. As No. 1620.

Rev. As No. 1620, but mint-mark, 　│＊
　　　　　　　　　　　　　　CONOB

N, 4.48 gm. ↓.

1623 Solidus Constantinople, AD 473–4

Obv. As No. 1620.

Rev. SALVS REIPVBLICAE. Leo I and Leo II, nimbate, seated facing, enthroned, each holding globe; between heads of emperors, cross, surmounted by star; mint-mark, CONOB.

N, 4.39 gm. ↓.

In AD 473 Leo I appointed as a fellow Augustus his grandson Leo II, son of his daughter Ariadne and Zeno, the *magister militum* who, it had been expected, would be Leo I's successor.

1624 Æ 2 Constantinople, AD 457–74

Obv. D N LEONIS P P A AVG. Bust, pearl-diademed, draped, cuirassed, r.

Rev. VIRTVS EXERCITI. Emperor standing r., holding standard in r. hand, and globe in l., with l. foot spurning captive; mint-mark, CONЄ. 5.71 gm. ↓.

For this denomination, see No. 1606.

1625 Æ 2 Constantinople, AD 457–74

Obv. D N LEO PRPET AG. Bust, pearl-diademed, draped, cuirassed, r.

Rev. SALVS RPVRLICA. Emperor standing r., holding standard in r. hand and globe in l., with l. foot spurning captive; mint-mark, CON. 3.71 gm. ↓.

Both obverse and reverse inscriptions show lapses in orthography.

1626 Æ 4 Constantinople, AD 457–74

Obv. D N LEO P F AVG. Bust, pearl-diademed, draped, cuirassed, r.; above head, cross.

Rev. Lion standing l., head r.; mint-mark,

　│＊
　CON

1.09 gm. ↓.

The reverse type is a pun on the emperor's name.

1627 Æ 4 Constantinople, AD 457–74

Obv. D N LEO. Bust, pearl-diademed, draped, cuirassed, r.
Rev. Empress enthroned facing, holding cross on globe in r. hand, and transverse sceptre in l.; in field l. and r., b– €; no mint-mark. 0.87 gm. ↓.

1628 Æ 4 Constantinople, AD 457–74

Obv. As No. 1627.
Rev. Within wreath, monogram ⱶÆ. 0.96 gm. ↓.

1629 Solidus Constantinople, AD 457–74

Obv. AEL VERINA AVG. Bust, diademed, draped, r.; above, hand of God.
Rev. VICTORIA AVGGGB. Victory standing l., holding long cross; mint-mark, $\frac{\quad|\;*}{\text{CONOB}}$.

N, 4.33 gm. ↓.
Coinage was issued by Leo for his wife, Verina.

1630 Æ 2 Constantinople, AD 457–74

Obv. As No. 1629, but no hand.
Rev. SALVS REIPVBLICAE. Victory seated r., inscribing Chi-Rho on shield set on column; mint-mark, CONE. 4.94 gm. ↓.

1631 Æ 4 Nicomedia, AD 457–74

Obv. D N LEOS P F AVG. Bust, pearl-diademed, draped, cuirassed, r.
Rev. Emperor standing facing, holding long cross in r. hand, and captive with l.; mint-mark, NIC. Æ, 1.22 gm. ↓.

Leo II and Zeno, AD 474

1632 Solidus Constantinople, AD 474

Obv. D N LEO ET ZENO PP AVG. Bust, pearl-diademed, helmeted, cuirassed, facing, holding spear over shoulder in r. hand, and shield in l.
Rev. SALVS REIPVBLICAE. Two emperors, nimbate, enthroned, facing, each holding globe; between heads, cross, surmounted by star; mint-mark, CONOB. *N*, 4.42 gm. ↓.

On the death of Leo I, after only a few days Leo II appointed his father Zeno as his fellow Augustus. The smaller of the two figures on the reverse is clearly Leo II with Zeno seated on his left, the conventional position of the junior of two emperors.

Basiliscus, AD 475–476

1633 Solidus Milan, AD 475–6

Obv. D N BASILISCVS PERT AVG. Bust, pearl-
diademed, helmeted, cuirassed, facing,
holding spear over shoulder in r. hand, and
shield in l.

Rev. VICTORIA AVGGG. Victory standing l.,
holding long cross in r. hand; mint-mark,

$$\frac{\quad | \ *}{\text{COMOB}}$$

N, 4.41 gm. ↑.

Zeno reigned alone after the death of Leo II, but in
early AD 475 was ousted by a palace revolution, and
replaced by Basiliscus, brother of the empress
Verina. At Milan coinage was struck for Basiliscus
as well as the last western emperor, Romulus
Augustus. PERT = Perpetuus

1634 Solidus Thessalonica, AD 475–6

Obv. As No. 1633, but P F instead of PERT.

Rev. As No. 1633, but mint-mark,

$$\frac{\quad | \ *}{\text{THSOB}}$$

N, 4.26 gm. ↓.

1635 Solidus Constantinople, AD 475–6

Obv. As No. 1634, but PP instead of P F.

Rev. As No. 1633, but officina letter A after
AVGG and mint-mark,

$$\frac{\quad | \quad}{\text{CONOB}}$$

N, 4.47 gm. ↓.

1636 Æ 4 Constantinople, AD 475–6

Obv. D N BA / / / AICTV. Bust, pearl-diademed,
draped, cuirassed, r.

Rev. Within wreath, monogram, ⳨. 1.00 gm. ↓.

Basiliscus and Marcus, AD 475–476

1637 Solidus Constantinople, AD 475–6

Obv. D N BASILISCI ET MARC P AVG. Bust, pearl-
diademed, helmeted, cuirassed, facing,
holding spear over shoulder in r. hand, and
shield in l.

Rev. VICTORIA AVGGGS. Victory standing
l., holding long cross in r. hand;
mint-mark,

$$\frac{\quad | \ *}{\text{CONOB}}$$

N, 4.42 gm. ↓.

Basiliscus appointed his son Marcus first as Caesar
and then as Augustus. The obverse carries only one
bust but two names expressed in the genitive.

1638 Tremissis Constantinople, AD 475–6

Obv. D N BASILISCI ET MARC P AVG. Bust, pearl-
diademed, draped, cuirassed, r.

Rev. VICTORIA AVGVSTORVM. Victory standing
facing, head l., holding wreath in r.
hand, and cross on globe in l.;
mint-mark,

$$\frac{\quad | \ *}{\text{CONOB}}$$

N, 1.46 gm. ↓.

1639 Solidus Constantinople, AD 475–6

Obv. D N ZENO ET LEO NOV CAES. Bust, pearl-diademed, helmeted, cuirassed, facing, holding spear over shoulder in r. hand, and shield in l.

Rev. VICTORIA AVGGZ. Victory standing l., holding long cross in r. hand; mint-mark,

$$\frac{\quad | \quad *}{\text{CONOB}}.$$

N, 4.42 gm. ↓.

The identification of the Caesars Zeno and Leo remains controversial. They were probably younger sons of Basiliscus who were nominated Caesar when Marcus was advanced to the rank of Augustus.

1640 Tremissis Constantinople, AD 475–6

Obv. D N ZENO ET LIEO NOV CAES. Bust, pearl-diademed, draped, cuirassed, r.

Rev. VICTORIA AVGVSTORVM. Victory standing facing, head l., holding wreath in r. hand, and cross and globe in l.; mint-mark,

$$\frac{\quad | \quad *}{\text{CONOB}}.$$

N, 4.40 gm. ↓.

This obverse was struck from an altered die which originally bore the name of Basiliscus and Marcus.

1641 Solidus Constantinople, AD 475–6

Obv. AEL ZENONIS AVG. Bust, diademed, draped, r.; above, hand of God.

Rev. VICTORIA AVGGGA. Victory standing l., holding long cross in r. hand; mint-mark,

$$\frac{\quad | \quad *}{\text{CONOB}}.$$

N, 4.47 gm. ↓.

Coinage was also struck for the empress Zenonis, the wife of Basiliscus.

Zeno, AD 474–475, 476–491

1642 Tremissis Rome, AD 490

Obv. D N ZENO PERP F AVG. Bust, pearl-diademed, draped, cuirassed, r.

Rev. Cross in wreath; mint-mark, ·COMOB·.

N, 1.41 gm. ↓.

Coinage in the time of Theoderic who visited Rome in AD 489.

1643 Bronze Rome, AD 489–91

Obv. INP ZENO FELICISSIMO SEN AVG. Head, laureate, r.

Rev. GLORIA ROMANORO. Victory advancing r., holding wreath in r. hand, and trophy over shoulder in l.; in field l. and r., S–C; in ex., XL. Æ, 16.69 gm. ↑.

A series of bronze coins, marked as 40 nummi, was struck by the Ostrogothic king Theoderic at Rome in the name of Zeno.

1644 Bronze Rome, AD 489–91

Obv. INP ZENO SEMPER AVG. Bust, laureate, draped, cuirassed, r.

Rev. IMVICTA ROMA. Victory advancing r., holding wreath in r. hand, and spear over shoulder in l.; in field l. and r., S–C; in ex, XL. Æ, 18.39 gm. ↗.

Another bronze coin of 40 nummi similar to No. 1643.

1645 **Solidus** Ravenna, AD 480–90

Obv. D N ZENO PERP AVG. Bust, pearl-diademed, helmeted, cuirassed, facing, holding spear over shoulder in r. hand, and shield in l.

Rev. VICTORIA AVGGG:. Victory standing l., holding long cross in r. hand; mint-mark,

R | V
COMOB
.

N, 4.38 gm. ↓.

1646 **Half-siliqua** Ravenna, AD 480–90

Obv. D N ZENO PERP AVG. Bust, pearl-diademed, draped, cuirassed, r.

Rev. Turreted figure to l., holding staff in r. hand, and cornucopiae in l.; mint-mark, R–V. Æ, 0.97 gm. ↓.

1647 **Half-siliqua** Ravenna, AD 480–90

Obv. As No. 1646.
Rev. Eagle standing l., head r. Æ, 0.93 gm. ↓.

1648 **Solidus** Milan, AD 476–80

Obv. As No. 1645, but inscription ends AⅤG.
Rev. VICTORIA AVGGG. Victory standing l., holding long cross in r. hand; mint-mark,

M | D
COMOB
.

N, 4.39 gm. ↑.

1649 **Half-siliqua** Milan, AD 480–90

Obv. As No. 1646, but inscription ends AG.
Rev. As No. 1646, but mint-mark, M–D.
Æ, 0.95 gm. ↑.

1650 **Half-siliqua** Milan, AD 480–90

Obv. As No 1646, but inscription ends AVG.
Rev. Eagle standing r., head l., on prow, wings spread; above, cross. Æ, 0.92 gm. ↑.

1651 **Solidus** Thessalonica, AD 476–91

Obv. D N ZENO PERP AVG. Bust, pearl-diademed, helmeted, cuirassed, facing, holding spear over shoulder in r. hand, and shield in l.

Rev. VICTORIA AVGGG. Victory standing l., holding long cross in r. hand; mint-mark,

* | *
CONOB
.

N, 4.47 gm. ↓.

1652 Miliarensis Thessalonica, AD 476–91

Obv. D N ZENO PERP AVG. Bust, pearl-diademed,
        draped, cuirassed, r.
Rev. GLOR ORVS TARRAR. Emperor, nimbate,
        standing facing, head l., holding spear
        in r. hand and resting l. on shield;
        mint-mark, ⸭| .
        ‾‾‾‾‾THSOB
        Æ, 3.84 gm. ↓ (pierced).

1653 Solidus Constantinople, *c*.AD 480

Obv. As No. 1651.
Rev. As No. 1651, but at end of inscription
        officina letter A; mint-mark,
        | ⸭ .
        ‾‾‾‾
        CONOB
        N, 4.45 gm. ↓.

The style of the obverse portrait is like that on coins
of Basiliscus (cf. No. 1635) and so belongs to the
earlier part of the reign.

1654 Solidus Constantinople, *c*.AD 490

Obv. As No. 1653.
Rev. As No. 1653, but officina letter H.
        N, 4.05 gm. ↓.

As the obverse portrait style is continued on coins of
Anastasius, the issue can be dated towards the end of
the reign.

1655 Semissis Constantinople, AD 474–91

Obv. D N ZENO PERP AVG. Bust, pearl-diademed,
        draped, cuirassed, r.
Rev. VICTORIA AVGGG. Victory seated r. on
        cuirass, inscribing shield held on knee;
        mint-mark, ⸭|✠ .
        ‾‾‾‾‾‾
        CONOB
        N, 2.22 gm. ↓.

1656 Tremissis Constantinople, AD 474–91

Obv. As No. 1655.
Rev. VICTORIA AVGVSTORVM. Victory standing
        facing, head l., holding wreath in r. hand,
        and cross on globe in l.; mint-mark,
        | ⸭ .
        ‾‾‾‾
        CONOB
        N, 1.49 gm. ↓.

1657 Æ 4 Constantinople, AD 474–91

Obv. D N ZENO / / / / / . Bust, pearl-diademed,
        draped, cuirassed, r.
Rev. Monogram Æ. 1.12 gm. ↓.

As with many late fifth-century Æ 4 coins the
obverse die is too large for the flan so that only
portions of the inscription are legible.

1658 Tremissis Constantinople, AD 474–91

Obv. AEL ARIADNE AVG. Bust, diademed, draped, r.
Rev. Cross in wreath; mint-mark, CONO⸭.
        N, 1.46 gm. ↓.

Coinage was struck by Zeno for his empress, Ariadne. Some of Ariadne's coinage may belong to the reign of Anastasius whom she subsequently married.

Anastasius, AD 491–498

1659 Solidus Thessalonica, AD 491–8

Obv. D N ANASTASIVS PP AVG. Bust, pearl-diademed, helmeted, cuirassed, facing, holding spear over shoulder in r. hand, and shield in l.

Rev. VICTORIA AVGGG. Victory standing l., holding long cross in r. hand; mint-mark,

$$\frac{* \mid *}{\text{CONOB}}.$$

N, 4.36 gm. ↓

Rare solidi of the early coinage of Anastasius from the mint of Thessalonica are distinguished by the use of two stars in the mint-mark.

1660 Solidus Constantinople, AD 491

Obv. D N ANASTASIO PERP AVG. Bust, helmeted, cuirassed, facing, holding spear over shoulder in r. hand, and shield in l.

Rev. VICTORIA AVGGG. Victory standing l. holding long cross in r. hand; mint-mark,

$$\frac{\mid *}{\text{CONOB}}.$$

N, 4.41 gm. ↓

Following the death, probably by murder, of Zeno, Anastasius was elected emperor, and shortly afterwards married the empress, Ariadne. His titles here are unusually given in the dative case. The solidi of the early part of the reign are distinguished by the continued use of a voided long cross held by Victory on the reverse as on the coinage of the preceding emperors. After AD 498 the cross on the reverse takes the form of a plain cross surmounted by ✚.

1661 Solidus Constantinople, *c.* AD 495

Obv. As No. 1660, but ANASTASIVS PP.

Rev. As No. 1660, but, at end of inscription, officina letter I. N, 4.48 gm. ↓

1662 Semissis Constantinople, AD 491–8

Obv. D N ANASTASIVS PP AVG. Bust, pearl-diademed, draped, cuirassed, r.

Rev. VICTORIA AVGGG. Victory seated r. on cuirass, inscribing shield held on knee; mint-mark,

$$\frac{* \mid ✚}{\text{CONOB}}.$$

N, 2.18 gm. ↓

The semissis which accompanies the early group of solidi is distinguished by the form of the cross in the mint-mark. In the later group the form is ✚.

1663 Æ 4 Constantinople, AD 491–8

Obv. D N ANASTA (SIVS PP AVG). Bust, pearl-diademed, draped, cuirassed, r.

Rev. Monogram ℟. 0.91 gm. ↑

This small bronze nummus is one of the last issues of this category.

1664 Bronze Constantinople, AD 498

Obv. D N ANASTASIVS PP AVG. Bust, pearl-
diademed, draped, cuirassed, r.

Rev. Constantinopolis seated l., r. foot on prow,
holding cross on globe in r. hand; to l., M;
to r., star; mint-mark, CONє. Æ, 17.86 gm. ↓.

An example of the new bronze coinage whose
introduction in AD 498 traditionally marks the end
of the Roman coinage and the beginning of the
Byzantine series. The letter M on reverse, the Greek
numeral 40, marks it as a piece of 40 nummi.

1665 Bronze Constantinople, AD 498

Obv. As No. 1664.

Rev. M surmounted by cross; mint-mark, CON.
Æ, 9.12 gm. ↓.

An example of the more typical bronze issued in
AD 498 with reverse consisting only of the value in
nummi expressed by the Greek numeral M.

Concordance

For Nos. 1150–1474 the reference given is to *RIC* (*Roman Imperial Coinage*, VI–IX, the reference number being preceded by the appropriate mint in abbreviated form. For Nos. 1495–1569 the reference for gold and silver coins is to Cohen (Henry Cohen, *Description historique des monnaies frappées sous l'empire romain, VIII*), and for bronze coins to *LRBC* II (*Late Roman Bronze Coinage*, Part II). For Nos. 1570–1665 the reference for gold and silver coins is to Tolstoy (J Tolstoi, *Bizantinckiya Moneti*), and for bronze coins, again to *LRBC*. References to such medallions which are not included in these works are given to Gnecchi, *I Medaglioni Romani*, I–III, abbreviated eg G I, p. 11, 6.

No.	Ref.	No.	Ref.	No.	Ref.	No.	Ref.
FIRST TETRARCHY		1187	3	1223	91	1261	Ser. 19
1150	Lon. 12	1188	38A	1224	278	1262	21
1151	17	1189	Sis. 12a	1225	Tr. 626a	1263	Thes. 32a
1152	NC 1930, p. 229	1190	10	1226	676b	1264	Her. 37a
1153	Tr. 36a	1191	17b	1227	627	1265	Nic. 44
1154	66	1192	34a	1228	638	1266	62
1155	87b	1193	57b	1229	730	1267	66c
1156	82	1194	121	1230	758	1268	39
1157	99	1195	Ser. 1b	1231	756	1269	Cyz. 102
1158	96	1196	4b	1232	789	1270	Ant. 69
1159	46	1197	Thes. 3	1233	812	1271	p. 627n
1160	86	1198	1b	1234	826	1272	Ant. 111
1161	102a	1199	14b	1235	VII, 212	1273	134
1162	105a	1200	26a	1236	VI Ly. 209	1274	140
1163	125	1201	Her. 17a	1237	286	1275	Alex. 52
1164	381a	1202	G I, p. 11, 6	1238	Tic. 54a	1276	61
1165	Ly. 176b	1203	Nic. 3	1239	103	1277	9b
1166	Tic. 7	1204	29a	1240	Aq. 41a	1278	144b
1167	27b	1205	9	1241	81b	**CONSTANTINE AND LICINIUS**	
1168	20b	1206	12	1242	R. 113	1279	Lon. 168
1169	43a	1207	25b	1243	136	1280	Tr. 8
1170	11a	1208	13	1244	137	1281	312
1171	Aq. 1	1209	6	1245	151	1282	435
1172	2a	1210	Cyz. 11a	1246	R. 172	1283	442
1173	16a	1211	18b	1247	21b	1284	443
1174	7b	1212	Ant. 8	1248	249	1285	473
1175	9	1213	15	1249	Cart. 48b	1286	Tr. 532
1176	37b	1214	43b	1250	51a	1287	Ly. 29
1177	R. 3	1215	54a	1251	53	1288	113
1178	8b	1216	Alex. 4	1252	71	1289	Arl. 31
1179	30a	1217	5	1253	Ost. 5	1290	50
1180	42a	1218	20	1254	11	1291	R. 104
1181	87a	1219	10b	1255	69	1292	264
1182	103b	1220	32b	1256	Sis. 170b	1293	G. II, p. 139, 10
1183	Cart. 1	1221	43	1257	153	1294	Tic. 25
1184	14a	**SECOND, THIRD TETRARCHIES**		1258	196	1295	53
1185	32b			1259	211		
1186	15b	1222	Lon. 59b	1260	232a		

1296	Aq. 27
1297	31
1298	36
1299	81
1300	Sis. 26
1301	204
1302	206
1303	234
1304	Sirm. 2
1305	60
1306	Thes. 71
1307	R. 146
1308	Her. 80
1309	Con. 19
1310	32
1311	63
1312	98
1313	108
1314	146
1315	Nic. 41
1316	42
1317	45
1318	89
1319	113
1320	195
1321	Cyz. 2
1322	Ant. 2
1323	cf. Her. 50
1324	Ant. 86
1325	104
1326	Alex. 68

SONS OF CONSTANTINE I

1327	Tr. 12
1328	21
1329	31
1330	R. 356
1331	Aq. 2
1332	Sis. 20
1333	61
1334	259
1335	Thes. 21
1336	10
1337	23
1338	Con. 17
1339	39
1340	34
1341	Ant. 25

CONSTANTIUS II, CONSTANS

1342	Tr. 129
1343	158
1344	175
1345	185
1346	234
1347	Ly. 80
1348	Arl. 62
1349	R. 62
1350	113
1351	153
1352	157
1353	385
1354	382
1355	Aq. 44
1356	63
1357	Sis. 145
1358	176
1359	Thes. 78
1360	Con. 90
1361	Ant. 75
1362	64
1363	112

CONSTANTIUS II, GALLUS, JULIAN

1364	Am. 2
1365	29
1366	Tr. 255
1367	268
1368	248
1369	293
1370	332
1371	347
1372	Ly. 119
1373	130
1374	Arl. 215
1375	239
1376	R. 177
1377	404
1378	409
1379	413
1380	202
1381	172
1382	441
1383	292
1384	298
1385	464
1386	Mil. 2
1387	Aq. 124
1388	145
1389	Sis. 260
1390	261
1391	292
1392	Sirm. 14
1393	Thes. 131
1394	179
1395	198
1396	Con. 100
1397	151
1398	Nic. 75
1399	99
1400	77
1401	80
1402	100
1403	161
1404	162

JULIAN, JOVIAN

1405	Tr. 362
1406	Ly. 208
1407	Arl. 304
1408	308
1409	Thes. 218
1410	Sirm. 104
1411	Con. 162
1412	Ant. 201
1413	204
1414	Thes. 229
1415	Con. 169
1416	176

VALENTINIAN I, VALENS, GRATIAN

1417	Tr. 1a
1418	13a
1419	16c
1420	17e
1421	21e
1422	22
1423	23a
1424	26a
1425	27e
1426	19
1427	12a
1428	39c
1429	Ly. 2
1430	3
1431	Arl. 4
1432	6a
1433	10a
1434	15
1435	17b
1436	Mil. 1
1437	R. 4b
1438	8
1439	Sis. 3b
1440	5b
1441	Sirm. 3
1442	Thes. 1
1443	Her. 7
1444	Con. 1
1445	5b
1446	8
1447	4
1448	29b
1449	cf. 26
1450	Nic. —
1451	16b
1452	Ant. 2d
1453	20
1454	22c
1455	14

GRATIAN, VALENTINIAN II, THEODOSIUS I

1456	Lon. 2b
1457	3
1458	Tr. 51
1459	56c
1460	76
1461	79a
1462	90b
1463	99
1464	105
1465	Ly. 25
1466	38a
1467	40
1468	44
1469	46
1470	Arl. 25
1471	29
1472	R. 33c
1473	37
1474	Mil. 15
1475	19a
1476	21a
1477	28
1478	35a
1479	Aq. 21d
1480	24
1481	Sis. 26b
1482	Sirm. 15d
1483	Thes. 34c
1484	44
1485	64d
1486	Her. 25
1487	Con. 45a
1488	49
1489	57b
1490	75a
1491	Ant. 39a
1492	41b
1493	67
1494	Alex. 18

HONORIUS

1495	NC 1959, p. 15
1496	C. 44
1497	32
1498	44
1499	57
1500	72
1501	44
1502	38
1503	60
1504	63
1505	15
1506	44
1507	LRBC II, 1144
1508	C. 44
1509	51
1510	43
1511	47
1512	12
1513	44
1514	69
1515	3
1516	46
1517	LRBC II, 2595

CONSTANTINE III

1518	C. 5
1519	2
1520	7

PRISCUS ATTALUS

1521	C. 3
1522	5

JOVINUS

1523	C. 1
1524	2

MAXIMUS

1525	C. 1

CONSTANTIUS III

1526	C. 1

JOHANNES

1527	LRBC II, 837
1528	C. 4
1529	9

VALENTINIAN III

1530	C. 34
1531	24
1532	LRBC II, 840
1533	845
1534	855
1535	(Eudoxia) C. 1
1536	C. 44
1537	(Placidia) C. 13
1538	C. 19
1539	48
1540	(Honoria) C. 1
1541	C. 46
1542	(Placidia) C. 5
1543	(Placidia) C. 16
1544	C. 9
1545	42
1546	—

PETRONIUS MAXIMUS

1547	C. 1

AVITUS

1548	C. 5

MAJORIAN

1549	C. 12
1550	C. 1
1551	LRBC II, 582

LIBIUS SEVERUS

1552	C.8
1553	2
1554	16
1555	LRBC II, 871
1556	C. 10

ANTHEMIUS

1557	C. 7
1558	19
1559	LRBC II, 874

EUFEMIA

1560	C. 2

OLYBRIUS

1561	C. 3

GLYCERIUS

1562	C. 2

JULIUS NEPOS

1563	C. 6
1564	16
1565	6
1566	13
1567	15

ROMULUS

1568	C. 3

JULIUS NEPOS (restored)

1569	C. 5

ARCADIUS

1570	cf. T. 52
1571	T. 57
1572	30
1573	—
1574	5
1575	136
1576	143
1577	149
1578	28
1579	LRBC II, 2442
1580	2580

THEODOSIUS II

1581	Sab. 22
1582	T. 36
1583	59
1584	Sab. 2
1585	3
1586	NC 1959, p. 15
1587	T. 9
1588	—
1589	T. 17
1590	(Pulcheria) T. 31
1591	T. 45
1592	cf. T. 40
1593	64
1594	cf. 58
1595	10
1596	33
1597	LRBC II, 2236
1598	98
1599	Sab. 15
1600	T. 61
1601	50
1602	74
1603	Sab. 21
1604	T. 37
1605	23
1606	LRBC II, 2231
1607	2592
1608	2599
1609	2928

MARCIAN

1610	T. 16
1611	1
1612	2
1613	19
1614	—
1615	23
1616	LRBC II, 2250
1617	(Pulcheria) T. 36

LEO I

1618	T. 45
1619	15
1620	14
1621	Sab. 11
1622	T. 9
1623	2
1624	LRBC II, 2253
1625	2254
1626	2258
1627	2272
1628	2264
1629	T. 52
1630	LRBC II, 2253
1631	2471

LEO II, ZENO

1632	T. 1

BASILISCUS

1633	cf. T. 83
1634	80
1635	cf. T. 73
1636	LRBC II, 2283
1637	cf. T. 89
1638	93
1639	5
1640	7
1641	cf. T. 94

ZENO

1642	cf. T. 52
1643	LRBC II, 875
1644	878
1645	T. 39
1646	60
1647	62
1648	41
1649	58
1650	61
1651	42
1652	—
1653	11
1654	21
1655	25
1656	29
1657	LRBC II, 2283
1658	T. 71

ANASTASIUS

1659	T. 78
1660	cf. 70
1661	76
1662	123
1663	LRBC II, 2288
1664	—
1665	T. 31

Indexes

1 Emperors and their relatives, etc.

The references are to coin numbers, not to page numbers.

II Mints

The references are to coin numbers, not to page numbers.

Alexandria, 1216–21, 1275–8, 1326, 1494, 1609

Amiens, 1364–5

Antioch, 1212–15, 1270–4, 1322–5, 1341, 1361–3, 1400–4, 1412–13, 1452–5, 1491–3

Aquileia, 1171–6, 1240–1, 1296–9, 1331, 1355–6, 1387–8, 1479–80, 1506, 1582

Arles, 1289–90, 1348, 1374–5, 1407–8, 1431–5, 1470–1, 1496, 1519, 1524, 1548, 1550, 1563

Barcelona, 1525

Carthage, 1183–8, 1249–52

Constantinople, 1309–14, 1338–40, 1360, 1396–7, 1411, 1415–16, 1444–9, 1487–90, 1515–17, 1544–6, 1574–8, 1586–1606, 1612–17, 1622–30, 1632, 1635–41, 1653–8, 1660–5

Cyzicus, 1210–11, 1268–9, 1321, 1580, 1607–8

Heraclea, 1201, 1264, 1308, 1443, 1486

London, 1150–1, 1222–4, 1279, 1456–7

Lyons, 1165, 1236–7, 1287–8, 1347, 1372–3, 1406, 1429–30, 1465–9, 1520

Milan, 1386, 1436, 1474–8, 1501–5, 1551, 1556, 1564, 1568–9, 1573, 1633, 1648–50

Nicomedia, 1202–8, 1265–7, 1315–20, 1398–9, 1450–1, 1579, 1631

Ostia, 1253–5

Ravenna, 1508–14, 1526, 1528–9, 1537–43, 1549, 1562, 1565–7, 1572, 1583, 1610, 1645–7

Rome, 1177–82, 1243–8, 1291–3, 1330, 1349–54, 1376–85, 1437–8, 1472–3, 1497–1500, 1521–2, 1527, 1531–6, 1547, 1552–5, 1557–61, 1570–1, 1618, 1642–4

Serdica, 1195–6, 1261–2

Sirmium, 1304–5, 1392, 1410, 1441, 1482

Siscia, 1189–94, 1256–60, 1300–3, 1332–4, 1357–8, 1389–91, 1439–40, 1481

Thessalonica, 1197–1200, 1263, 1306–7,
1335–7, 1359, 1393–5, 1409, 1414, 1442, 1483–5, 1584–5, 1611, 1619–21, 1634, 1651–2, 1659

Ticinum, 1166–70, 1238–9, 1294–5

Trier, 1152–64, 1225–35, 1280–6, 1327–9, 1342–6, 1366–71, 1405, 1417–28, 1458–64, 1495, 1518, 1523, 1530, 1581

III Types

The references are to coin numbers, not to page numbers.

Africa, stg. l., 1183–4, 1251

Altar, lighted and garlanded, 1232; surmounted by globe, 1281

Anthemius and Leo I, stg. facing, 1557

Arcadius, stg. r., 1494; and spurning captive, 1572; stg. facing, head l., 1492, 1570; and crowned by Victory, 1580

Arcadius and Honorius, both nimbate, std. facing, 1573

Arles, as turreted figure, receiving Moneta, 1289

Avitus, stg. facing, foot on human-headed serpent, 1548

Bull, stg. r., 1411

Camp-gate, 1534; open door and two turrets, 1291, 1471; three turrets, 1195, 1199, 1214, 1219, 1262; four turrets, 1207, 1228, 1230, 1268; eight turrets, 1178

Carthage, stg. facing, head l., 1250

Christogram in wreath, 1539, 1543, 1553–4, 1558; flanked by alpha and omega, 1565, 1570

Cippus, inscribed, 1289

Concordia, std. l., 1122, 1240; stg. l., 1275–6

Constans, stg. l., 1337; on galley, 1350; and Constantine II, stg. facing, in consular dress, 1361

Constantine I, stg. l., 1227, 1237, 1287, 1245; in consular dress, 1307; veiled, 1363; with three sons, 1318; advancing r., 1302; riding l., 1296; riding r., 1233; in quadriga r., 1339

Constantine II, stg. l., 1286, 1304; riding r., 1330; and Crispus, confronted busts of, 1300; with Constantius II, and Constans stg. facing, 1335

Constantine III, stg. r., 1518

Constantinopolis, std. l., 1546, 1605; with letter M to l., 1664; std. facing, head r., 1485, 1487, 1489, 1515, 1524, 1579, 1584, 1586–7

Constantius I, stg. r., crowned by Victory, and raising Britannia, 1152; riding r., 1160

Constantius II, stg. l., 1329, 1331, 1359, 1394, 1397; stg. r., 1285; with two captives, 1360; stg. r., with Victory, 1378; std. l., 1399; riding r., 1401; spearing two barbarians, 1351; in

IV General

The references are to page numbers.